The Home Renovation Bible

By Margaret Hart

Published by the Sovereign Media Group.

iii

PART TWO

PART THREE

INTRODUCTION

For the last 20 years I have bought, renovated, developed and sold property in the USA, UK and Australia and I have made a very good living! It has kept me out of the nine-to-five, given me the freedom to travel, to take time off as I see fit and pursue a life that I love, all while delivering me a good passive rental income.

Whether you are buying your own home, building a rental portfolio or flipping investment properties, dealing in real estate can be hugely profitable; but it is not a sure fire fool proof money spinner. You need to know what you are doing. If you get it right you will set yourself up for life, get it wrong and you could loose everything.

Picking a winner is both an art and a science. The science is in crunching the numbers, doing your research, knowing your market and knowing what problems not to buy into. The art is in imagining what is possible and making it happen for less.

While the basic principals of minimising risk and maximising return are quite simple, there is no magic formula on how one does that. Every property will present you with its own unique set of problems and potentials and must be thoroughly assessed on its own merits, a process that can be quite frightening to the uninitiated. There are literally hundreds of decisions to be made and each one will have a bearing on how successful your project is.

The Home Renovation Bible brings together over 20 years of experience from across the globe to create a comprehensive guide to buying, renovating and selling houses. It is not just a typical "How to DIY" book, *(although there is plenty of that included)*, it is a reference manual providing detailed information on how to pick a profitable deal from a financial sink hole; how to effectively plan and cost your projects, and how to avoid the all the common *(and some not-so-common)* traps that bring down many inexperienced players.

Armed with the information contained in this book you will be able to move forward confidently, without fear, knowing that you are asking the right questions, making the right plans and taking the right action for your future success.

Good luck and enjoy the journey!

Margaret Hart

For Mike and Suzanne, for sharing my life and love.

And putting up with my power tools and paint

trays all over the house

A note to my American friends:

While there is much information contained in this book that is quite specific to the USA, this is an international publication and as such I have chosen to write it in British English, as it is my native language. Please don't be offended when I spell colour with a "u", or if you see an "s" where you think it should be a "z". I can assure that in spite of being presented in UK English, the information provided herein is just as valuable and relevant to those living in the Americas as it is to those living in the UK or Australia or anywhere else for that matter.

PART ONE

GETTING READY TO BUY

SETTING YOUR STRATEGY

The first thing you need to know is that working with real estate is a marathon, not a sprint. So don't rush! Great deals are like buses; if you miss one there is always another one coming. Real estate can be a costly game and it is far better for you to take your time, do your research, build up your knowledge base and set your strategy before you enter the market.

As a starting point there are several things you should consider before you start hunting for bargains, such as:

1. Do you intend to keep the property and rent it out, or sell it on?

2. Are you intending to live in the property?

3. What are your preferred locations?

4. What is your proposed budget and borrowing capacity?

All of these factors can and will influence the choices you make, so it's good to be very clear on your strategy right from the start. I would suggest you start a notebook for each project and dedicate the first page to answering these questions.

DO YOUR RESEARCH

There is an old adage in real estate...

"You make your money when you buy"

And it's true! If you buy well that's more than half the battle. I recently purchased a property for $180k that was listed at 25% below current market value, so even if I turned it around and put it straight back on the market I could expect to make $53K profit *(after costs)* for less than a day's work.

Admittedly those kind of deals don't come along everyday and when they do you have move fast. That property was on the market less than one day before I snapped it up. But if you have done your research you will know a bargain when you see it; and if you have your finance in place you can feel very confident in moving quickly.

It is absolutely critical to your success that you know your market. When looking to buy into an area you need to assess everything: shopping, schools, transport, owner to tenant ratios, crime, walkability, environment etc. What is happening in the neighbouring areas? Are they up and coming? What is happening with populations? Are they growing or declining? What are the employment options in the area? Are plants and industry closing or are new businesses opening up? Is it commuting distance to more expensive areas; like the home counties are to London, or New Jersey is to New York?

Most real estate websites have a large amount of sales and market data that you can access for free. In addition to generalised information such as median price, search volumes, long-term growth trends and suburb demographics etc., some sites have lists of recent sale prices within a suburb and some sites even have a comprehensive database that will tell you when and for how much a particular house last sold for.

I recommend getting hold of the statistics for *"days on market"* if you can. This will be very useful information if you are planning to renovate and sell a property, because if houses are taking six months or more to sell in your area that is definitely going to have an impact on your holding costs*. If these stats are not readily available in your area you will be able to get a fairly good idea by talking to local realtors and keeping an eye on the local sales listings. It doesn't take too long to figure what is moving and what is not.

Your holding costs are what it costs you in mortgage payments, council taxes and utilities etc. to have the property sitting there vacant.

Most real estate web sites will let you set up an email alert that will message you immediately whenever a new property that meets your requirements is listed for sale. Once you have decided exactly what it is you are looking for it is definitely worth setting up an alert, so you can be right there when a bargain hits the market. This is how I found the house I mentioned above that was listed at 25% under its market value.

Check regularly to see what has sold for what price in your area and what is still sitting on the market. Sometimes a house that has been priced incorrectly, presented poorly or marketed badly can go stale on the market. People often think if a house has been on the market too long there must be something terribly wrong with it. But don't automatically dismiss a property just because nobody else seems to want it. There may be a very good reason a house has been hanging on the market, but I have bought many highly profitable properties that have sat on the market for 8-10 months or more, *(and in one case 2 years)*. If a property has been sitting around for a long time the vendor can get very despondent and will be more inclined to entertain a low-ball offer. Often you can get a real bargain.

When assessing whether a property represents good value don't just go by the median price for the suburb. Make sure you know the whole area as there can be a wide variation in price, amenity and resale potential even within one zip/post code. Is there a right and wrong side of the tracks? Are there water views in one street and semi industrial in another? Was part of the suburb once council or public housing? All these things can skew the statistics on an area and have a huge impact on a property's value. I have one property that I purchased for 40% under the suburb's median value. While it was undoubtedly a bargain it is an ex-council house - a fact that actually accounted for about 20% of the apparent price anomaly.

Talk to the local real estate agents, pick their brains. But be mindful, while most realtors are honest and straight up not all of them will tell you the truth, however if you speak to enough of them you will start to get a fairly accurate picture of what is happening in a particular market.

Sometimes a house has been the scene of some famous local crime, or was a noted brothel, or a drug lab. I once had a bank teller ask me if a house I had just bought was "the murder house", *(the murder house was actually 2 doors up, but all the locals knew about it)*. Buying a "murder house" or a house that was a brothel or a drug lab right up until last week could very easily ruin your chances of a good resale. Conversely if you are going to pull it down and rebuild, or do an extensive twelve-month renovation there is a good chance you can rehabilitate the property's reputation, and the discount on the asking price is just more cream for you. Be wary though, while notorious properties can be real cash cows you need to ask a few more questions and apply both rigour and common-sense in assessing the costs and benefits of acquiring a such a property.

For example: houses that have been used as drug labs can have high levels of toxic contamination and may require expensive remediation to become habitable again. I have heard of people being required to remove and replace all the plaster and floor boards in order to remove toxic residues. It is worth noting that not all drug-lab houses are on skid row, sometimes they are in top-notch neighbourhoods, so even if you are looking in an expensive area it pays to ask.

When you are seriously considering purchasing a particular property always make sure to email the agent and ask if the house has a history, or if there anything you should know about the property. If you ask, they are legally obliged to tell you. There was a high profile case recently in Australia where an overseas purchaser was able to back out of a purchase contract for a multi million dollar property and gain compensation because neither the vendor or the agent disclosed a multiple homicide that had taken place on the premises. While the law on this varies quite a bit from place to place, if you email the agent, and insist they also put the question to the vendor it will serve as proof that you have asked and any failure to disclose should allow you some recourse.

KNOW ALL YOUR COSTS

The price of a property is not just the price on the contract plus what you spend on the renovation. There are many fees and charges that can throw your budget out, including: legal fees *(closing costs),* mortgage application fees, stamp duties, valuation fees, completion fees, registration fees, realtor and agents fees, advertising, photography, plans and permits, inspection fees, property/council taxes, utilities and holding costs etc.

While it is impossible to predict all these costs with 100% accuracy, once you have ascertained all the associated costs in your jurisdiction, you should have no trouble estimating within a 10% margin of error. *(Although holding costs can vary greatly depending on how long it takes you to turn over a property, so make sure you allow a generous contingency).*

GET YOUR FINANCE SORTED

This may seem fairly obvious, but I can't tell you how often I talk to people who want to buy a property, have seen something they like, and only then race off to a lender to see if they can get the money. More often than not they miss out because they either cannot afford it, they have some minor stain on their credit history, or it simply takes too long to get an answer out of the bank and someone else beats them to it.

Talk to the bank or a mortgage broker first, before you start looking seriously. Find out how much you can borrow and how much it will cost you to service that loan. Get any paperwork, such as tax returns, wage slips and references in place so you can get your finance pre approved. That way when a killer deal pops up you are ready to act immediately.

Most mortgage brokers do not charge you a fee, as they make their money in commissions from the lenders. A good mortgage broker will know under what circumstances which banks will lend what, so if you have anything slightly unconventional *(like being self employed)* as part of your application I recommend using a broker. The chances are that someone you know has used a good mortgage broker so ask around for recommendations.

It is worth checking your credit rating for any outstanding anomalies that may scuttle your deal. I have known people to miss out on a property because of a $60 utility bill that they accidentally missed when moving house years earlier. There are many companies that can help you clean up your credit rating, so if you have a patchy credit history start working on getting it fixed NOW.

WHAT KIND OF LOAN?

Principal and interest loans

The most common type of loan is a principal and interest loan *(sometimes referred to as a repayment or PI loan)*. With a PI loan each repayment you make is made up of an amount of the actual loan sum *(the principal)* plus interest. Usually at the start of the loan you pay very little off the principal, in fact the amount you owe the bank often doesn't seem to go down at all for the first few years. If you are hoping to pay off a property it is better to pay off as much of the principal sum as you can as early as possible. This type of loan is often best for a home you intend to live in for a long period, but make sure there are no penalties or charges for making extra payments.

Tip: You can save tens of thousands of dollars on a PI loan if you schedule your payments for weekly or fortnightly instead of monthly. The bank will often not mention this as they make a lot more money if you pay monthly, so make sure you ask your bank or broker for information about this.

Interest only loans

The monthly repayments on an interest only loan *(IO loans)* can be significantly cheaper than for a PI loan, which can help your cash flow position and allow you to borrow a little more. This can be very helpful when you are trying to make a deal work.

IO loans can be especially good for long hold rental properties, as most often you do not pay off much principal in the first five to ten years, but you can get significant capital growth in some markets. The cheaper repayments of an interest only loan can enable you to benefit from that capital growth without compromising your cash flow too much.

IO loans are also much better for quick renovate and sell properties. As you would not be expecting to pay off more than a few dollars in principal over a typical 3-6 month renovation period, having cheaper repayments during your renovation will put less strain on your budget.

Home equity loans

If you already have substantial equity in your own home, you may be able to get a line of credit secured against your house, ensuring that you can act quickly and pay cash when a wonderful opportunity presents itself.

*While the ability to pay cash puts you ahead of most other potential buyers it is crucial that you understand that there are risks involved in taking a line of credit over your house. If the project runs into to trouble, or you become unable to complete the project and are forced to sell it at a loss you will be left *carrying the outstanding debt.*

Off set loans

While not technically a loan, an offset facility is a feature that some loans offer whereby any interest calculated and charged on the loan is reduced by the amount of money you hold on account. For example if you have a loan for $100k, but you currently have $20k in a designated bank account, the loan interest would not be calculated on the full $100k you owe, but rather on the $100k less the $20k you have on account, meaning your interest would only be calculated on $80k.

This type of feature is particularly good for paying off your own home. Many people put all their wages and income into their offset facility as it adds up to a significant saving over time. That said, offset facilities are not available in all places or from all banks so you will need to ask your bank or broker if this option is available for you.

Off panel lenders

If you find you are having trouble with the banks due to troubled credit or a patchy income record there are "off panel" lenders that may lend to you at a higher interest rate. This is obviously not your first choice but it can be good for some people who otherwise would not be able do a deal. These loans often attract steep application fees, higher interest rates, early break fees *(if you refinance within a certain time period)* and exit fees. While these loans can be very helpful, read the fine print carefully and make sure you know all the costs associated with the loan. Any good mortgage broker should have information and access to some off panel lenders.

I currently have one "off panel" loan that has an interest rate 1.2% higher than the market average. I took that loan out as I was living in a different country at the time and was unable to prove relevant income details to the bank *(being a foreign tax resident at the time)*. As soon as the "early break fees" no longer apply I will refinance the property down to a market interest rate.

The loan to value ratio

The loan to value ratio (often referred to as the LTV or the LVR) is the percentage of a property's value that has a mortgage over it. For example if you bought a house with a 20% deposit and borrowed 80% of the purchase price. That property would have an LTV of 80%, simply meaning that you have borrowed 80% of the value.

After assessing your file a lender will usually tell you at what LTV they are prepared to lend to you at. I have known banks offer to lend at LTV ratios as high as 95%, and as low as 60%, depending on the borrowers circumstances. It is best not to assume that because your friend borrowed 90% of the purchase price that you will be able to. Talk to your bank or broker and find out what your LTV is most likely to be.

Lender's Mortgage Insurance

In some circumstances you will be required to take out lenders mortgage insurance, (also known as a "higher lending charge" or "mortgage indemnity guarantee" in the UK). This is a one time upfront payment made at the time your mortgage is activated. As a rule of thumb the higher the LTV the more likely it is you will be asked to take mortgage insurance.

While the name "mortgage insurance" implies you are insured in case you have any missed payments that is not the case. Even though you pay for it, mortgage insurance is actually there to provide insurance cover for the bank or lender, not you. If you want to cover yourself in case of accident or missed payments you will have to take out income protection or mortgage payment protection insurance (MPPI).

Traps to avoid

In many countries having a mortgage application refused will show up on your credit file for some time to come, and can act as a red flag for any other lender you may apply to. Once you have had an application rejected by one bank, other banks may refuse to lend to you simply because someone else has knocked you back. If you are not careful this can have a snowball effect, where the more your applications are rejected, the more your applications are rejected.

It is best not to apply if there is any doubt about whether your application will be accepted. If you are concerned about it I strongly recommend using a good broker. However if you have had an application refused it is not the end of the world. If you are upfront with a lender about a previous refusal, are able to explain why it happened, demonstrate that the problem was an anomaly *(not part of an ongoing pattern),* and that the issue has now been fully resolved, many lenders will be satisfied and happy to take your business. A good broker will know which lenders are more likely to overlook such issues.

Honeymoon interest rates are another thing to watch out for. Often lenders will offer a mortgage at a very low, "teaser" interest rate for a period of maybe one or two years. The "honeymoon rate" is far lower than the rate you will end up paying, so if you intend to hang onto the property make sure you do all your rental yield and repayment calculations based on the higher interest rate.

Variable versus fixed interest rates

This is a difficult question to answer and what you ultimately choose will depend on your circumstances. Fixed rates offer a lot of security and certainty, but are often not suitable for renovate and flip* deals as they can have heavy penalties if you cash out before the fixed period expires.

"Flipping" in an informal term for buying, fixing and selling a house within a relatively short time frame.

Variable rates can change drastically in a short period of time and some less than scrupulous lenders will exploit market fluctuations.

As a rule of thumb I would go for fixed rate if I intended to own the property for a long period and rates were low at the time of fixing. I would go for a variable rate if it is a short-term deal or if interest rates where unusually high at the time.

I remember seeing people fix their interest rates at 13 -15% for as long as five years during a very dark period in Australia when interest rates went to a short-term peak of 17%. These poor souls who fixed their interest rates at 13-15% watched helplessly as rates dived back down to 7%. They were totally stuck, as the terms of their fixed mortgages required them pay huge exit fees to get out of their contracts. Many of them went bankrupt and lost their homes.

PLAN YOUR TAX

There are many different taxes that can apply to a property deal and you need to know what they are and how to plan for them. Stamp duties, council/property tax and water rates cannot be avoided or minimised. But the taxes you pay on the sale of a property can be planned for to ensure you are not paying any more than you need to.

While I am unable to offer region specific advice, *(as each country and state has its own laws)*, there are some general principals that hold true in most jurisdictions. You can use this information to assist you in asking your accountant the right questions. If you do not ask the right questions you will not get the tax benefits that you are entitled to. Asking the right questions is key to effective tax planning!

The following passage is general information and is not intended to be taken as advice. I highly recommend you talk to an accountant to get detailed advice that is relevant to your particular location and circumstances.

Your own home

Your own home, *(your principal place of residence),* does not usually attract any tax on sale and as such you are free to keep all the profits.* This may vary in certain countries so make sure you check your local laws. In the USA for example, there is a threshold where you only pay capital gains tax on your own home after the first $250,000 profit for an individual, or $500,000 for a couple filing jointly.

* *With regard to your own home the profit would usually be deemed to be difference between the price you sell your home for and the price you paid for it, plus the cost of any fees, stamp duties, closing fees, renovations and improvements plus any sale costs such as agents fees, advertising and legal work.*

Many people have used the tax-free nature of their own home to renovate, sell and move on a reasonably regular basis, pocketing a fabulous return in the process. While you can technically renovate and on sell your own home every year there are countries *(such as Australia)* that view the practice as tax evasion and have laws against doing it too often, *(although what is "too often" is frequently ill defined and subject to the whims and interpretation of the prosecuting taxation authority)*.

If "trading in your own home" is against the law in your area, and you are found to be engaging in this practice you can be deemed liable and forced to pay back taxes on previous sales. While regularly renovating and selling your own home can be very profitable given the risks involved I would not recommend doing this more often than once every 3-4 years.

Investment properties

There are many different structures you can use to buy and sell real estate. You can use your own name, a limited liability company or a trust. Each structure has it's own implications in terms of your tax and contingent liability.

For example company tax rates in the UK are around a flat 20%. If you are in a high-income bracket it may be better to use a company to buy and sell property. I suggest you talk to your accountant and do some research on what structures are available in your jurisdiction and how they might best meet your needs.

With investment properties there are, for the most part, two ways they can be taxed on sale. One is as income; the other is a capital gain. Most often capital gain, *(the profit you make by selling and investment that you have held for a certain period of time)* is the lesser tax, although that is not always the case, *(particularly in the UK)*.

In most places you must hold the asset for at least one year for it to be taxed as a capital gain. If you only hold the asset for a short time then any profit you make will be taxed as income, as if it were part of your wage, *(or earnings from company or sole trading)*. Depending on your income bracket this could be anywhere from say 15 - 49 cents/pence in the dollar/pound for an individual or sole trader. If however you own the property in a company or a trust it would be taxed at the standard company/trust tax rate, *(unless the company or trust has the provision to "pass through" income to a nominated third party for tax purposes, which is a provision that many trusts and certain USA company structures have)*.

If you buy a house, renovate it quickly and resell it within a year it will generally be treated as income, where as if you held that property for one or two years and then sold it would be taxed as a capital gain. Sometimes, particularly if you are in a high income bracket, it can be worthwhile renting the property out for a year before renovating and selling so you can be taxed at the lower rate.

There can also be implications for sales tax, *(also known as state tax, VAT or GST)*, when holding property for longer or shorter time frames. For example if you buy and sell quickly, and are thus taxed on your earnings as income you may be able to claim back any sales tax you have paid out in the course of the project. Once again the laws on this vary from place to place but it is worth talking to your accountant about sales tax and finding out up front what reimbursements or liabilities your project might attract.

Tax authorities often treat money spent on repairs differently to money spent on improvements. If you plan to hold a property long-term you may need to account for money spent on the property in one of two different ways: as repairs and ongoing maintenance or capital improvements.

For example: if the kitchen tap breaks and you have to replace it that would be taken as a **maintenance expense** against any rental income, and be written off in the same financial year.

If however you decided that the kitchen was out of date and replaced it that would be viewed as a **capital improvement**, and would be treated as part of the capital cost *(the price you paid for the property)*, Some capital improvements, such as new carpets, blinds, stoves, bathrooms, kitchens etc. can be written off over several years as part of a *depreciation** schedule. Once again you will need to check your local laws to see what is allowed.

*Depreciation is the means by which you can write down a capital expense over several years. For example if you put new carpet in a rental property you may be able to write down 10% of it's value each year for a prescribed number of years.

Many people fail to claim depreciation on their rental properties and thus pay far more tax than they need to. Claiming depreciation on rental properties can significantly improve your bottom line so I highly recommend getting professional advice for your particular circumstances.

INSURANCE AND ASSET PROTECTION

Insurance

There are many things to be mindful of when purchasing and insuring a property, but the most important thing is that you **NEVER LEAVE A PROPERTY UNINSURED**, not even for one day! And it is always advisable to insure it immediately a contract goes unconditional. *(Do not wait for closure or settlement)*

Make sure you are not under insured: Insurance companies do not want to pay out and will look for anyway they can to reduce their liability. Example: If you are insured for $300K replacement costs, but the replacement cost is actually $400k and disaster strikes, as you are technically underinsured by 25% insurance companies have been known to argue that you are only insured for 75% of value so they only need to pay out 75% of the policy. In this example you would only get $225k on your $300k policy.

Make sure your insurance covers trades people working on your site: I recommend checking that all contractors you engage carry their own insurance, but none the less you want to be covered if there is an accident on site and there is a problem with their insurance. Check this with your insurers, as not all policies will cover contractors.

Make sure your insurance covers uninvited guests: Building sites and empty houses are magnets for neighbourhood kids and if one of them breaks into your property and breaks his leg you can still be liable.

Make sure you understand what the exclusions are: While storm damage is usually covered, flood damage from rising water is often excluded. Wild fire cover may be excluded or have special conditions, such as proximity of trees and the provision of fire plans and precautionary measures attached to it. **Know what the hazards are in your area** and make sure you are adequately covered.

Title Insurance

Title insurance is a must in the USA, as not all states hold reliable accessible title records and as such there is often no government guarantee that the title deeds you are looking at are in fact genuine. Also as some of the sale contracts in the USA are very light on detail and as a buyer and seller often use the same *closing agent (something I would not recommend)* there is more room for unscrupulous operators to scam unwary purchasers.

*A **closing agent** is the USA term for someone who acts on behalf of a buyer or a seller to facilitate the exchange of contracts,* *conduct all necessary searches and due diligence and execute the title and funds transfer. In the UK, Australia or NZ you would engage a solicitors or a conveyancer to perform these tasks.*

While problems and fraud are reasonably rare, title insurance is not expensive and it's well worth it to know that you will not be out of pocket if you get unlucky. Check that any title insurance you are purchasing is with a reputable company.

Title insurance is much less common in places like the UK and Australia as their governments keep comprehensive land registries and all sale contracts must provide government verified evidence of title as part of the contract disclosures. Also the practice of buyer and seller using the same closing agent *(AKA: solicitors or conveyancer)* is not permitted in many places as it is deemed to be a conflict of interest.

That said there have been cases where properties have been sold out from under unknowing owners by scammers who rent a house and then put it up for sale by impersonating the owners. The sale can appear legitimate to the realtor and the conveyancers as the title is in order, the sellers have convincing fake ID and no one realises that the sellers are imposters. The victims of this are mostly absent and overseas landlords who are not even aware that their property has been put up for sale.

This is a relatively new scam and how the situation will ultimately be resolved through the courts is still somewhat up in the air, but suffice to say there is a good chance the unsuspecting purchasers will lose the house and be substantially out of pocket. Once again title insurance is not expensive and would cover you against any losses should you to fall prey to such a scam.

Asset Protection

Know what a contingent liability could cost you. Anything can happen, and insurance will not always cover you. When considering what entity to buy a property in *(eg: your own name, a company or a trust),* consider what other assets that entity holds.

Example: you own your own home in your own name and you buy and investment property in your own name. Your tenant trips on the carpet and sues you, but your insurance says that the carpet was dangerously worn and it was neglect on your part that caused the accident and therefore they will not pay. The tenant could easily sue you and take your own home.

If however you had bought that property in a limited liability company or a trust that is administered by a company the tenant would not be able to sue you personally and thus any liability would be limited to whatever assets are held in that particular entity.

Companies and trusts have different provisions in different territories, so if you have personal assets you wish to quarantine from any potential liability you will need to do some research. It is possible to protect your assets with forethought and planning, and by making sure you purchase your properties in the correct structure for your particular circumstance.

Many people have gone personally bankrupt, yet because they have chosen to use an entity *(such as a company or a trust)* to actually buy their assets *(and as such they are not the legal owner of those assets)*, those assets do not form part of any personal bankruptcy settlement.

Clever asset structuring is how so many multi millionaires can go belly up but never seem to lose their shirts. If you plan to acquire and hold a lot of property then buying those properties in the right structures can provide good protection from bankruptcy or any other contingent liabilities that may arise. Working this out takes some skill however, and I would recommend you get professional advice.

ACTION POINTS

1.Do your research

2.Define your search criteria

3.Set your overall budget

4. Clean up your credit rating

5.Get your finance pre approved

6. Register any required companies or trusts

PART TWO

BUYING A PROPERTY

CHOOSING THE RIGHT PROPERTY

Choosing the right property is best the way to ensure your success. You will need to do some serious research to define your search area and be clear about what type of property you are looking for. Do not rush this process. It takes time to understand a market, the peculiarities of a particular area and its growth potential.

Choosing your location

Naturally, there will be very different issues at play depending on what your intention is for the property. If you intend to live in a property you will have a vastly different set of requirements than if you are buying it for a rental investment, or to renovate and on-sell. While your choice of where to live will be largely informed by your personal preferences you should still keep one eye on value-adding potential and a good resale profit down the track.

If you are buying for rental you need to consider things like rental demand, vacancy rates, rental yields, crime rates, owner to tenant ratio (you want a good proportion of owner occupied homes in the area) and tenant demographics. Do you intend to be self-managing the property or will you place it with a letting agent? And if you plan to place it with an agent is there a reputable letting agent in the area?

You will need to seriously assess what you can afford against your risk appetite before deciding the best place for your long-term rental investment. Generally the lower the socio-economic status of the tenants in a particular area, the higher the head line rental yield. In a down-market neighbourhood you may get a 6-12% yield where as in an upmarket neighbourhood it may be as low as 2-3%.

Rental yield is only one part of the equation. The capital growth outlook in a better neighbourhood can be much greater and this can more than compensate for the lower headline rental yield. Also down-market neighbourhoods have higher rates of rental delinquency and tenant damage, which can easily wipe out any apparent gain on yield. If you only have enough money to invest in a less expensive area then you need to pay careful attention to the type of tenant your property is likely to attract. You don't want to be buying yourself trouble. If however you can find a rental property in a low crime area that has had a good tenant in place for many years then you can expect a fairly trouble free run.

If you are buying to live, or to renovate and sell then mid level areas that are up and coming usually offer the best return. Areas next door to a "hot" suburb, or areas where there have been a very high percentage of elderly people that are now moving into care are always worth a look. These areas are often repopulated with young families who are keen to invest time and effort into rejuvenating their new neighbourhood and your property may get some good uplift in value off the back of their renovations.

Look for areas that have plateaued in value yet have a lot of valued amenities like good schools, shopping, restaurants and transport links. Often a suburb where the prices have not moved much for years will suddenly become popular and the prices will shoot through the roof. It is quite common for property values in a particular area to flat line for a few years and then spike, rather than stepping up incrementally. If you can identify an area that has the right mix of desirable housing and amenities, where prices have not moved for a few years, there is a good chance it is due for spike in price.

That said you should make sure there is nothing other than fashion keeping the prices low; no environmental or crime issues, no plans for a six lane highway to go through, no large employer shutting down. Conversely keep your ear to the ground for up and coming infrastructure developments that are likely to add value to an area. If you get in ahead of the curve you can get good capital growth out of slated redevelopment and infrastructure spending.

Top-end areas are very sensitive to price fluctuations and market sentiment and as such do not tend to be so good for investment purposes. Top end properties will fall a lot further a lot faster if the economy takes a turn. The lower middle and aspirational middle areas really are the sweet spot for lower risk and higher returns.

Do you really need to be in the best street?

If you are buying a house to live in it, it is perfectly understandable that you want the best possible street. But if you are buying to renovate and sell or to add to a rental portfolio is it really that important? Often people with a limited budget, who are not up to renovating themselves but are keen to live in a particular suburb will buy a renovated house on a main road because it is all they can afford in the area.

The significantly reduced buy-in price for a "renovators delight" in a less than optimal street often means you can make more money on the deal than you would from a house in the best street. Conversely hopeful first homebuyers often bid up un-renovated houses in the best streets to the point where they are not really financially viable as investor projects.

It is worth bearing in mind that rental properties on a main road don't necessarily demand a lesser rent than those in better streets; in which case a cheaper buy in price can simply mean a greater rental yield for you.

A house or a condo?

In some places, like Manhattan, Amsterdam or Berlin, practically everyone lives in an apartment and there are very few houses, so the choice is pretty well made for you; but in most urban markets you have a choice.

Apartments can offer a great entry into the property market, but personally I like houses for investment. Unless a house is heritage listed or subject to an owners association or a neighbourhood covenant you are pretty well free to do what you want with it, whereas a condo will often have strict rules about what you can and can't do.

If you are considering buying an apartment there are many issues you need to be mindful of in making the right choice. Everything from the age of the building, the security, the owner to tenant ratio, the monthly maintenance fees, building covenants and upcoming repairs to whether it is a leasehold or freehold title etc. In some places lenders have rules about minimum floor areas, so even the size of a unit can have a bearing on whether or not you can even get a decent mortgage on the property.

When buying a condo in the USA there can be a lot of additional hurdles such as condo board approval and finance restrictions. For example FHA will not lend for a condo in a building that is less than 50% owner occupied and other lenders may charge you a premium on your interest rate if the owner occupancy is low.

Then there are the maintenance charges, and it's not just the monthly fees you have to worry about; condo boards will often raise "special levies" to fix big problems. Some buildings are better managed than others, and put money away in a "sinking fund", so there is money available to cover unforeseen repairs. If you are planning on buying a condo you should look through the minutes from previous board meetings to find out if any big repairs are coming up. You should look into the building's finances to see if any money has been set aside to cover any repairs or unforeseen costs. You should also check that the building's insurance and public liability cover is in order and that there are no outstanding claims against the building.

Another issue with condos is buying into a ghost building. This is most common when you are buying one of the first units off the plan, but it has also been known to happen with foreclosures. When too many units are sitting vacant it will pull down the value of the building. It can happen because a developer fails to sell sufficient units, too many units have been foreclosed on or a building has too many owners that are financially stressed and not paying their dues. All of these scenarios can result in too few owners paying their share of the ongoing maintenance costs, which can result in just a handful of owners being forced to pay hugely inflated maintenance charges.

In boom times many people buy off the plan at the start of a new development with the intention of on-selling the unit just before completion and hopefully pocketing a good capital gain in the process. While some have made good money doing this, others have lost their shirts. This strategy is a highly risky proposition as there is no guarantee that the market will hold or that the building will be finished to an acceptable standard.

The recent apartment construction boom in cities like Toronto has left many buyers lumbered with sub standard, unsaleable units in a saturated market. As sales have slowed many developers have cut corners and lowered overall building standards to try and mitigate their losses on unsold inventory. There have been cases of off the plan purchasers being forced to close on units where the plumbing doesn't work and doors don't even close properly. There have also been many cases of purchasers not being able to close on a unit because the lender no longer considers it a viable security, in which case the buyer forfeits their deposit and may be sued for breach of contract by the developer.

Buying a bargain

There are several factors and a range of different circumstances that can make it possible for you to bag a bargain property. For example: getting in quick, buying a property that has gone stale on the market, buying from a stressed vendor who is desperate for a quick sale; buying at auction; buying a property with a hoarding tenant; buying a property with a questionable history; buying a half done renovation or even buying a property with a bad smell.

I once bought an old butchers shop with a dwelling attached.

The vendors had not cleaned out the cool room properly and the place stank to the point of retching. The property sat on the market for 2 years. Eventually I bought it for less than 1/2 its market value. I had the cool room removed the day I picked up the keys and the smell went with it. You do need to be careful though. Some bad smells, like urine, can seep into the floorboards and you may have to replace the floor to get rid of it.

Sitting tenants, rent controlled and rent stabilised apartments: When hunting down a bargain property with a tenant in place be very careful to fully review the lease, as they may have rights as a **"sitting tenant"** (UK). This means the tenant has the right to occupy the property for the rest of their life and can pass that right of occupancy on to another family member in their will. A house with a sitting tenant is often priced well under market value and as such it can appear to be a bargain, but you may never be able to do anything with it, and selling it will not be easy. Sometimes you can pay a sitting tenant to vacate but is not uncommon for a sitting tenant to demand tens of thousands of pounds to leave.

There are also places in the USA with similar potential restrictions on landlords. For example, New York's rent-control program limits the rent an owner can charge for an apartment and may restrict an owner's right to evict a tenant.

The program applies to residential buildings constructed before February, 1947 where the tenant has been in place since before July 1, 1971. Some rent regulated units offer tenants succession rights, which mean they can pass the tenancy on to their heirs.

When a rent-controlled apartment is vacated, it either becomes rent stabilized or completely removed from regulation. If it is removed from regulation then you will win big time; if not you will have an investment you cannot fully capitalise on.

Each rent-controlled apartment has a maximum base rent that is adjusted every two years to reflect changes in operating costs. Tenants may challenge rent increases if the landlord exceeds the legal regulated rent, the building has housing code violations, the owner's expenses do not warrant an increase, or the owner is failing to maintain essential services.

Avoiding a money pit

Ultimately what you want is the property that has the most potential and will cost the least to renovate. That property is most often one that is structurally sound but "decor challenged". While structural problems are not necessarily deal breakers they do need to be fixed, *(it's not wise to ignore them as they will probably come back to bite you when your buyer gets a building inspection done).*

The main problem with fixing structural issues is that unlike putting in a fabulous stainless steel kitchen with moulded stone countertops, they chew up your budget but often add nothing to your sale price. Structural problems can be expensive to fix, and the money you spend just brings you up to the starting line, you will still have to do the renovation on top of that.

If a property has one or two such issues but is otherwise very promising then you might consider it, *(as long as you know what it will cost you to fix it and you are absolutely sure you have the funds)*, but if a property has several of these issues then proceed with caution. Unless you are very experienced renovator I would steer clear as you could be buying a money pit.

The following is a list of structural issues and big-ticket items you should look out for as they can really blow out your budget.

1. Foundations

Concrete cancer:

If the property is on a concrete slab and there is evidence that the slab is crumbling this is pretty much a deal breaker unless you intend to demolish the house. The costs involved in fixing such problems are huge and will most likely blow your budget. Steer well clear of this one.

The one exception to this rule would be for old sunrooms, conservatories and lean-to extensions. The concrete floors in these structures are often crumbling, twisted and broken because they were built over garden paths or patios and as such the concrete often lacks the depth and reinforcement required to support a structure. It is often necessary to rebuild a sunroom or lean-to extension, *(something that is not usually prohibitively expensive)* and most of the time any cracked or crumbling concrete can be quite easily broken up and removed. You can then either replace it with fresh concrete or a sprung floor *(a sprung floor is a floor that is on stumps and joists)*.

Re-Stumping:

(Also known as reblocking) As a general rule only lightweight constructions such a timber houses are built on stumps*. If a house is built on stumps sometimes you may need to replace one or several of them, and this is usually evidenced by a sagging in a corner or a bouncing in the floor.

* Stumps are a collection of concrete or wooden posts that are set into the ground to support the weight of a building.

If the whole house looks crooked then you probably need to re-stump the entire property, which can be expensive, as it requires jacking up the property, digging out the old stumps and putting in new ones. Re-stumping a whole house often requires a permit from the local authority and you will probably be required to use registered professional re-stumpers.

If the house is quite low to the ground it is not always possible to get under the house to jack it up. In such cases you will have to remove the floor in order to re-stump. Generally the floorboards do not survive this so you will need to budget for a new floor.

If a house is too low to the ground *(or even on the ground as I have seen more than once)* it may have issues with rising damp or rot in the frame, and it may not even be possible to raise it up enough to get adequate ventilation under the floor. Unless you intend to demolish it I would avoid any house that is too close the ground as it is likely to be a never-ending money pit.

On the other hand if the house has enough height for sufficient underfloor ventilation *(I would want at least about 10 inches or 25 centimetres)*, and it only has a few stumps that need replacing, *(this would be a house that seems to sag in one corner or has moderate floor bounce in one or two places)* then quite often your carpenter will be able to replace the stumps and fix the problem without too much drama or expense.

If the house is crooked or sagging you should have a look around and see if you can spot an obvious cause for the problem. You may find that there is an issue with a clogged gutter or downpipe leading to the ground being saturated, which has in turn caused the stumps to rot. There may also be tree roots that are causing problems.

Sometimes a house that is on stumps will have a few brick piers, or a fireplace that is founded on concrete or brick, which can settle differently leading to cracking walls and uneven floors around the fire hearth. This is usually not too big a deal to fix but get professional advice.

Many old houses are on wooden stumps *(which are subject to rot)*, but today's stumps are made of concrete, so once you have fixed the problem and replaced any bad stumps the problem is unlikely to re-occur. If the stump problems are limited to just one or two areas I wouldn't be put off buying the property.

If you are going to have any stumps repaired or replaced then make sure your builder or re-stumper installs ant caps to protect you from the possibility of termite damage in the future. They are very cheap, usually no more than one or two dollars each but they provide good protection against future termite damage.

I actually had a sale fall through once because a house didn't have ant caps and the purchaser's building inspector frightened the buyer so much about it that they pulled out of the sale. Ironically, the house was built long before ant caps were even invented. It was a brick house that was over 150 years old; it was not in a termite prone area and had never had any termites in it. The floor was Cyprus pine (which termites hate) so the likely hood of a termite attack was extremely low, but I still lost the sale.

Underpinning:

Underpinning is the process of reinforcing or replacing strip foundations* under a brick structure.

The process usually involves digging out the existing foundation, jacking up the brickwork and re-building a new damp course and concrete foundation. Digging out the old foundation can be difficult and may require costly measures such as <u>vacuum excavation</u>. Underpinning a brick or stone property could easily run into tens of thousands of dollars.

* Unlike a concrete slab, a strip foundation is a narrow strip of concrete, brick or stone that is dug down into the ground to support the weight of the outer walls. Houses on strip foundations may also have stumps or piers under the body of the building to support the floor.

If a building seems to be visibly sagging in places or there are large openings in the brickwork take this as a warning that you could be in for some very expensive repairs. I would definitely get professional advice before purchasing a property in this condition.

That said a certain amount of cracking and movement will occur in all houses and hairline cracks are not necessarily a sign of any major problem. Are you in an earthquake zone? Cracking may be a normal part of living in such an area. Sometimes a very hot dry summer or an unusually wet spell can cause the soil around a building to swell or contract leading to some movement.

You should also check for issues with gutters or storm water that could be causing problems such as soil erosion. If the property is on a hill you should check for any signs of slippage or subsidence, as this can be a seriously expensive problem to fix. If you are in any way unsure I would get professionals in to inspect the problem and give you a quote for any repairs that would be required.

Underpinning is considerably more difficult and costly than re-stumping and generally speaking I would avoid a house that needed underpinning.

Note: with any re-stumping or underpinning you may have to repair or replace the internal plasterwork, as the process of fixing the foundation often causes the walls to crack.

2. Timber framing, cladding and flooring

Termite damage and rot are the most common issues with timber framing, cladding and flooring.

If you are in an area that is subject to termites it is wise to pay for a pest inspection before you purchase. While a small amount of termite damage is not usually a huge problem a house that is totally riddled with termites may not be able to be saved. It is quite common for people to put a clause in a sale contract that stipulates that the sale is subject to the results of a pest inspection; if the house subsequently turns out to be termite infested you can back out of the purchase without penalty.

Timber rot can be "wet" or "dry". Wet rot is most common in cold, damp or very humid climates, and can be accompanied by some rather nasty moulds and mildews. Dry Rot is more often found in hotter more arid climates. Rot can be caused by a lack of proper maintenance, such as not keeping the paint work in good order, problems with guttering or drainage, moisture seepage from unsealed baths and showers, leaky plumbing in wall cavities or *(as mentioned in the previous section)* inadequate sub floor ventilation.

Sometimes rot in timber can be quite obvious, but it can also be difficult to detect on initial inspection. You should check any windows, accessible floorboards and cladding for any signs of wood that looks flaky or uneven. Press your finger into the wood; if it pushes in easily and collapses under your fingers you probably have some rot *(or possible termite damage)*.

As long as the house is not too close to the ground, rot is usually a localised problem. Once you have remedied the cause *(such as a lack of paint, problems with gutters, inadequate sealing of bathroom tiles etc.)*, and filled or replaced any rotten timber you discover you are usually OK. I would not be put off buying a place with minor rot issues, but at the risk of repeating myself I would steer clear of a house that is too low to the ground.

3. Brickwork and render

The main issues associated with brickwork are rising damp, porous brick and sandy or crumbling mortar.

Rising damp:

Rising damp is not pleasant to live with and can render a house uninhabitable if it is bad enough. It can produce toxic moulds and induce asthma and allergy attacks. The tell tale signs of rising damp are mould spots, flaking paint and salt damage on the walls, *(salt damage is caused by salts leaching out of the brick work, it looks a bit like your walls are suffering from a bad case of acne).*

If the damp is caused by something like rusted out or split pipes, or blocked or inadequate storm water drainage resulting in the brickwork absorbing large amounts of moisture, it can often be remedied quite cheaply. You just need to identify and fix the cause of the problem. Once you have done this there is a good chance that over time the bricks will dry out, and while you will still have to repair the damaged plaster, the actual problem will be resolved.

*Note: North facing walls, (or south facing walls in the southern hemisphere) may take considerably longer to dry out depending upon the climate, temperature and light level.

If the rising damp is due to issues with the damp course*, or if the house is very old and has no damp course, then the problem can be a little trickier to fix. Installing or replacing a damp course can involve digging out the foundations so it can be just as costly as underpinning. There are a few cheaper solutions but they are often ineffective and you can end up having to have it redone.

*(A dampcourse is a waterproof barrier built into the foundations to prevent damp from rising into the brick)

Whether or not you should buy a house with this kind of damp issue would depend largely on the level of the problem and how difficult it is to fix. I would recommend you get professional advice and at least one quote before you commit to purchasing such a property.

Porous bricks:

Some damp issues are caused by porous bricks, which is where the brick is not impervious to moisture and frequent exposure to storm water or rain causes the bricks to become saturated. This is quite a common problem in old houses in wet climates.

While many of the symptoms of porous brick are the same as for rising damp, they tend to be evenly distributed over the entire wall, as opposed to rising damp, which tends to only affect the bottom 1/3 of a wall.

Porous brick is not difficult to fix. Once you have attended to any contributing problems *(such as gutters and drainage)*, you can apply a sealer that forms a moisture barrier and prevents the brick from taking in any more moisture. This is best done late in the summer when the bricks are at their driest, as you don't want to be sealing moisture into the brick.

Sandy or crumbling mortar:

As the mortar is quite literally what holds the bricks together sandy or crumbling mortar can cause major structural problems.

If crumbling mortar is let go too far it could lead to a dangerous collapse.

The best way to identify crumbling mortar it is to pick a few different spots and run your finger along the mortar lines. If the mortar is loose and crumbling you could have a problem. This is particularly a problem with lime mortar used on houses built before 1900.

A word about ivy: ivy may look lovely climbing up your wall, but it just loves to pull the mortar out of your brick work. If you are looking at house that is covered in ivy take extra care to check the mortar. A small bit of ivy damage can probably be repaired but too much is a definite red flag.

If you do find a problem with the mortar and the issue appears to be localised check for any apparent cause. If the cause can be easily remedied it's not usually too difficult or expensive to get small areas of brickwork re-mortared. I would get a few quotes up front because prices for brickwork can vary widely depending on how common brick is in your area.

Note: Never re-mortar bricks without removing the old material or repairing the underlying problem. The outside of the repair may look good, but the mortar and brick underneath will continue to crumble.

Rendered finish:

Most rendered buildings are brick underneath but in recent years many new substrates have come onto the market. A rendered finish could be set over fibrous cement sheeting or even fire resistant polystyrene blocks, so do not assume that just because a building has render work that there is brick underneath.

Occasionally people render over cracking brickwork which has come about as the result of foundation problems. Usually rendered walls are absolutely fine, but you should be aware that render is sometimes used to conceal big problems in the brickwork and foundations.

4. The Roof

As well as damage to plaster, paint and carpets, roof leaks can lead to rot in the *roof trusses** Rot in the trusses can cause a roof to sag. A sagging roof is a sure sign that the roof has structural problems.

*Roof trusses are the triangular frames that support a pitched roof. In most homes they are timber but they can also be steel.

Whether the problem is too big to overcome is something that you may need to get your building inspector or surveyor to assess for you. If it is just one or two timbers that need replacing then it is probably quite Ok, but anything too much more than that and you should get some solid quotes or steer well clear.

There are many different types of roof designs, such as mono pitched roofs *(also known as skillion roofs)*, gable roofs *(also known as pitched roofs)* and flat roofs. Quite aside from the design there are also many different types of roofing material and each one can have potential problems.

Tiled roofs:

Terracotta or concrete tiled roofs are very common in some places, and while I would never knock back a house simply because it has a tiled roof, they are not my favourite.

Tiles are heavy, often difficult to match if you need to replace one, and they are easily cracked and broken by trades people that need roof access. I have had to repair several tiled roofs after having a TV antennae or satellite dish installed.

Tiled roofs are also prone to lichen and moulds, *(although to be fair in some climates everything is)* which can lift tiles, crack mortar joints and lead to spot leaks. That said, it is not stupidly expensive to get a tiled roof pressure cleaned, re-mortared and repainted and when you do it will look like a brand new roof.

If your tiled roof is sagging and the trusses are clearly under stress, will need to get the trusses shored up. It may also be worth considering replacing the tiles with a lighter weight material like metal tiles or corrugated roof steel. *(Steel is quite a common roofing material in many places, but in some places, like the UK, they just don't use it).*

Slate and shingled roofs:

Shingled roofs are very common in Europe and North America. They can be made of a variety of materials, and can vary a lot in weight. If you are replacing a shingled roof, you need to be certain that your roof trusses and timbers are strong enough to take the weight of the new shingles. If you are increasing the weight of your shingles, *(by going from asbestos to slate for example)* you may need to budget for reinforcing the roof trusses. There are however many wonderful new lightweight shingles available so do your research as to what is available in your area.

Depending on the climate most shingled roof have about a 20-30 year life span before they need to be looked at for potential problems, but some may last a lot longer. You should give the roof a thorough visual inspection, paying particular attention to any missing or out of place shingles and any flashings that look buckled or otherwise compromised.

A tip for shingled, slate and tiled roofs:

If you secure a couple of lengths of copper wire across the roof at the ridge line it will react with the rain to discourage lichens and moss from growing on your roof. It is not usually visible from the street and it can save you a lot of maintenance.

Note: Checking the roof is difficult if it is covered in snow, so it may be better to wait until the warmer weather.

Thatched roofs:

Thatched roofs are an undeniably cute and a much loved feature in many British towns. While I love the look of them, as an investor I am not a fan. They have a short life span (around 15-20 years), they attract insects and wildlife, they are difficult to clean and very expensive to replace. And as very few young people are taking up the thatching trade they are going to get considerably more costly to replace as time goes on.

Many thatched roofed houses have heritage listings so you will not be able to replace the roof with any other material. They are also very prone to fire, so a definite no-no if you like your open fire or if you are a smoker!

Metal roofs:

Personally I love a metal roof. I always choose a metal roof when building, *(if it is something that is done in the area)*, as they are relatively trouble free, come in a fabulous range of colours, are long lasting, cheap and easy to repair and I think they look fantastic.

There is a large range of styles and profiles, everything from ridged or corrugated sheets to traditional tile and shingle replicas.

Flat tar roofs:

Flat tar roofs are definitely not appropriate for high snow areas.

While they seem very popular in the less snowy parts of the east coast of the USA, *(I have seen a lot of them in New York),* people do not like them in the UK, and installing one may put off any potential buyers.

I have to confess I do not have a lot of experience with flat tar roofs. I have only owned one property that had one and I had no real trouble with it. The one time I had to make a repair it was a very simple procedure. I purchased a tin of roof tar from the hardware store and painted it on where there was a small leak. It was a very cheap, easy and effective fix.

Gutters, soffits, down pipes and storm water:

While gutters, soffits, down pipes and storm water drains are not major costs in a substantial renovation, they are often the source of many problems. If there are any problems at all with your storm water management system you will need to budget to have these items fixed. There is no way around this.

A word of warning on box gutters:

A box gutter is a U shaped guttering channel that runs over the top of a building's roofline, *(as opposed to a gutter that is mounted on the outside edge of a building).* Box gutters are not that common in older properties but have recently become quite popular with some architects as they can enable them to design sharp straight parapets on all sides of a building.

While architects may wax lyrical about the aesthetics, box gutters can be no end of trouble to maintain. If they become blocked or leaky you will end up with water inside the building and most probably damage to plaster, paint and carpet.

Fixing a boxed gutter is not always easy, and it can take several attempts to find and stop any leaks. If you are buying a house for the long term, or building an extension be aware that if it has a box gutter you will probably have issues with it at some point. I avoid a box gutter where ever possible.

5. Plumbing, Electricals and Asbestos

While plumbing, electrics and asbestos are not strictly speaking structural issues I am including them here because they need to be taken care of and like the structural issues outlined above, the money you spend getting them in order will not add a cent to your sale price.

Electricals:

Rewiring can be expensive, so if you see a lot of very old light fittings, switch plates and power points know that you are probably going to have to spend some money on the electrics. In most places it is illegal to do your own electrical work, and you will need to provide buyers with compliance certificates to show the work has been performed by an accredited professional. Even if it is legal to do your own electrical work in your area, you should still get it done by a professional. Amateur electrical work can be very dangerous and a lot of real people have died because of it!

If a house you buy is not fitted with a **safety switch*** I highly recommend that you have one installed the day you get the key. They are not expensive and if you have any wiring problems at all a safety switch will keep your tools safe, and keep you alive. This is particularly important in places like the UK, Australia and New Zealand where the power supply is 220-240V, as that kind of voltage can easily kill you. While it may be a little more difficult to kill yourself with the 110V power supply in USA, you can still give yourself a very nasty jolt, so **get a safety switch installed!**

*A safety switch is a circuit breaker that will cut the power instantly it detects any problem on a circuit. Say for instance you accidently cut into an electrical wire, it will instantly cut the power so you cannot electrocute yourself.

Plumbing:

You should turn on all taps and check for water pressure, leaks and pipe rattle. If a house is left vacant in a place where the winters are particularly cold and the plumbing has not been adequately winterised, *(winterising is a process of introducing anti-freeze into the plumbing system),* water can freeze and swell inside the pipes causing them to split. This can cause utter chaos in a property, as you can end up with a lot of water damage when things warm up and the ice starts to melt. It is often not possible to replace damaged pipes without hacking into the walls and floors, so your repair bills are not usually limited to the plumbing.

Sometimes vacant houses have the water turned off at the meter. You should always insist on turning it back on and checking for leaks, however if the pipes have been winterised this may not be possible. *(Along with snow preventing roof inspections, this is just one more thing that can make buying in the winter months far more risky).*

There have been big problems in the USA in recent years with vacant houses having their plumbing and wiring stripped out by thieves who sell the copper for scrap. While the signs that this has occurred are usually obvious *(holes in the walls and floors etc.)*, sometimes it's just the metal that is easily accessible that has been taken. If buying a vacant property either make sure you have it checked out or that you have the budget to replace whatever may be missing.

The hot water service *(or boiler)*: I have had to replace the hot water service (HWS) in pretty much every property I have ever bought. Sometimes you can get lucky and score a house with a relatively new one, but not often. I would take it as a given that if you own the property for more than a couple of years you will most likely have to replace the HWS at some point.

Central heating is essential in some places, so if a house doesn't have it, know that you will have to install it. If a house does have central heating you should check that it works, even if it is the middle of summer, *(The same applies to air conditioners in winter).*

Asbestos:

In many parts of the world asbestos has been banned in construction for many years. There can be strict guidelines for the handling and disposal of asbestos and often it can require permits and expensive professional removal.

Most people think of asbestos as something that is just found in the old fibrous cement sheet but there are many other places that it can be found in old homes. For example, old Linoleum, vinyl tiles, laminates, fake timber siding *(the cement sheet not the aluminium)* and fake brick cladding often contain asbestos, so if you are in any doubt you should take a small sample to your local environmental lab for testing.

Asbestos is generally considered safe if it is not disturbed and thus it is not always necessary to remove asbestos during a renovation, but you should always enact good safety protocols when asbestos is present. Wear an appropriate facemask and disposable overalls and wet down any asbestos surfaces to avoid raising any dust whenever you are removing or working around asbestos.

A vacuum cleaner should not be used to clean up asbestos as the small fibres can pass through the filter and become airborne making it much more dangerous.

You should never sand, drill or cut a surface you suspect to contain asbestos and you should wash any clothing exposed to asbestos dust immediately. Once again if you are in any doubt, get a professional inspection and ring around to find out what the likely cost of removal will be.

BUILDING INSPECTIONS AND REPORTS

There are many levels of building inspections *(AKA "Surveys" in the UK)* and reports and the price and quality can vary widely. Before you commit to a building inspection I suggest you ask the inspector what specifically they look for *(get a written list)* and have a clear list of questions you want answered.

Find out what level of guarantee they will give you, and if there is any recourse if they miss an obvious but costly problem. This is particularly important for pest inspections, as severe termite damage may not be able to be repaired, and can render the property unsafe to occupy.

Bear in mind however that the higher the level of accountability the more terrifying *(and expensive!)* the building report is likely to be, so when you actually get your building report try to stay calm. There are some inspectors who seem to think it is their job to scare you so much that you never buy anything *(and of course the more houses you reject the more building reports they get to sell you).*

Unless something major is uncovered I would try to balance a building report with professional quotes and advice. Sometimes what can look absolutely terrifying on the building report is really an easy and inexpensive fix, or simply nothing much to worry about.

Know that a building report will not necessarily uncover all the problems. An inspector can not pull up the carpet or pull the siding off the house so be prepared for the fact there may be some issues present that they simply can not detect.

The more houses you renovate, the less you will rely on building reports. As your knowledge and experience grows you will come to know what can be fixed easily and what is going to break the bank. Personally I have not had a building report done for many years as I am experienced enough to spot problems and know what they will cost to fix.

PRIVATE SALE OR AUCTION?

There are a number of different ways that properties can be offered on the market, the most common being auction and private sale. In the last few years however some other types of sales such as "sealed bid" *(AKA sale set date),* "call for expressions of interest", "vendors terms" and "rent to buy" have started to become far more common.

Private sales:

Put simply a private sale is where a vendor puts a price on the property and a purchaser offers to buy it either at or near that price. In most markets the asking price is usually higher than the price the vendor is actually expecting to sell for, so it is quite normal for a buyer to make an offer that is under the asking price. But if there is a lot of competition for a particular property offers can easily go well over the asking price.

In some places, like Scotland houses are listed with a base price, inviting "offers above". If a property is listed with an "offers above" price you are unlikely to buy it for under the listed price unless the seller is desperate or it has been on the market for a very long time.

Selling agents will always try to give the impression that there are one or several other buyers that are "hot" for the property, but this is not always true. Usually factors such as the temper of the market *(bull or bear),* and the length of time the property has been for sale will provide a good indication as to whether the agent is being honest about any competition you face.

There are two main methods of securing a private sale contract, and which one applies will depend on the laws of the state or territory you are buying in.

Contract Exchange: The buyer and seller agree a on price, then the buyer arranges for any building or pest inspections, gets their mortgage approval, engages a conveyancer or closing agent to conduct all necessary due diligence and searches such as a title search, previous planning and building permits, any liens or easements, or any potential threats to the title *(such as a* *proposed road widening for example).*

The contract exchange method is used in England and due to inefficiencies in the English system buyers can take up to two months getting ready to exchange, pay no deposit and then simply change their minds and walk away. This is a very common occurrence. I once had a "hot property" that I had to sell 4 times over a six month period before a buyer finally settled the deal.

Conversely in the regions of Australia where contract exchange is used any searches, inspections and approvals are usually completed within one or two weeks and contracts move very quickly to exchange. In Australia it is not at all uncommon for another buyer to come along and "gazump" you, *(make a higher offer and buy the property out from under you)*, so purchasers are usually very keen to move fast.

Straight Sale Contract: Straight sale contracts are common in the USA, and are used in certain parts of Australia and in Scotland. Once a price is agreed, and a *settlement period** is established, the buyer and seller sign and date the contract and the contract is immediately enforceable, *(unless there is a statutory* <u>"cooling off"</u> *period, which is often 3 days).*

*(The settlement period is the period between your signing the contract and the actual transfer of titles and your taking possession of the property. It is most commonly 60 days, but this is usually up for negotiation and can vary enormously).

Special contract conditions: Both buyers and sellers can have conditions inserted into the contract, such as a *subject to satisfactory building and pest inspection* clause, or a *subject to finance** clause.

*(A "subject to finance" clause is a provision that is used in some territories that allows a purchaser a set time to get a mortgage approved. If for what ever reason the purchaser is unable to get their mortgage approved they can legally withdraw from the contract and have their deposit refunded).

A word of warning with regard to your finance, even if your mortgage is pre approved the bank will still require the property to be independently valued. Even if you think you do not require a subject to finance clause as such, you should always have a *"subject to satisfactory bank valuation"* clause inserted into a contract, as this will cover you in the event that the bank values the property below the contract price.

Vendors will often be more inclined to accept an *"unconditional"* offer, than an offer that has a subject to finance clause attached, *(even if the unconditional offer is slightly lower)*, but most vendors will accept a *"subject to satisfactory bank valuation"* clause in an otherwise unconditional contract.

If you are buying with a mortgage you should ALWAYS insist that a *"subject to bank valuation"* clause be part of any unconditional offer you make.

I also like to add a *"subject to due diligence"* clause. This is very helpful if you need to go and see the local planning authority to find out if you can actually do what you have planned for the property. It is also a fairly loose clause and whether is it satisfied or not is based on your subjective opinion. It can be an excellent means of getting a property off the market for a few days while you adequately assess its potential.

Such clauses and conditions will usually have a time limit written in, most commonly *within 14 Days*, but if a purchaser needs a bit more time the vendor will usually grant them a few extra days.

If you are asking for a time extension on a clause or condition always make the request in writing, *(and retain proof, such as any emails you may have sent)*, otherwise the vendor could assert that the conditional period is over and the contract is unconditional before you are ready to fully commit. However if you can prove you asked for an extension this will cover you until you get the vendors response.

Auctions:

In the USA and UK auctions tend to be viewed as something for low end, fire sale properties and thus they attract lower prices. This can offer great opportunities for renovators and bargain hunters. On the other hand in Australia all the most promising properties go to auction, and auctions are considered the normal way to sell in the major cities.

As a buyer the main difference between auction and private sale is that the auction sale is final. Once the hammer falls the property is yours. No further inspections, no waiting to exchange contracts, no cooling off period, no *"subject to finance"* clauses. An auction sale is an unconditional, no ifs buts or maybes and if you fail to complete the sale you will lose your deposit, and may even be sued for breach of contract.

While banks in Australia have no problem lending to people purchasing at auction that is not the case in the USA or the UK, where comparatively few financial institutions will lend money for a property purchased at auction. Mostly you will need to pay cash to buy at auction in the UK or the USA.

Auction tips: The most important thing when buying at auction is to set your upper limit and stick to it. The adrenaline rush of auctions can cause people to get carried away and bid over their limit. NEVER DO THIS! If you are worried that you might do it get a trusted friend to bid for you.

Most often people set their bid limit on numbers ending in 0 or 5, if your limit is the same as another bidder's it is pure chance who's bid falls on that number. Where as if you had set your limit at say $201k instead of $200k for example, in most cases you will win the auction. It is always best to set your upper limit to a number ending in 1,2,3 or 6,7,8.

As the auction slows down or approaches your limit, offer bids in smaller increments. If the auctioneer is asking for another

£1,000, offer another £500, or £250. The Auctioneer will usually accept the bid and this can slow down the bidding and reduce the ultimate sale price.

If you plan to buy at auction go to as many auctions as you can before hand so you get used to the process and will not feel so overwhelmed or intimidated on the day. Make sure you have had any inspections or surveys done prior to the auction date. The agents are usually more than happy to arrange access.

A word of warning on buying with finance at an auction: *While most lenders will take the auction price as fair market value and not require a further valuation that is not always the case. Even if your loan is pre-approved the bank may still want to value an auction purchased property.*

This actually happened to my sister once and the valuer ticked the wrong box on the valuation form, marking the property as uninhabitable, (it was unrenovated but certainly not uninhabitable). As a result of the valuer's error the bank refused to give her her PRE-APPROVED loan. As she had bought at auction and thus had no "subject to finance" clause she was faced with loosing her deposit. Fortunately she was able to borrow the money from family and friends until she could get the mess sorted out with the bank, but it could have been a real disaster.

Sealed bids and set date:

Prospective buyers seal their best offer in an envelope and submit it to the estate agent. On a nominated day all the bids are opened and the highest bidder gets the property.

If the market is buoyant and the property is highly desirable this method of sale usually works in the vendor's favour. At times people get emotionally attached to a property and submit a bid well over what is a reasonable price or what they would have negotiated in a private sale.

If there is little interest in the property, or the market is quiet, it will favour the buyer. Unless a seller is desperate for a quick sale, sale by set date is not something you would usually see in a depressed market.

In a sealed bid situation it is important to discuss any clauses or conditions you want in the contract, such as a "subject to finance approval" clause or a shorter or longer settlement period before you submit your bid.

Expressions of interest:

This method of sale is quite rare and is usually reserved for expensive, high-end properties. Run down properties sold this way are usually sitting on a large or valuable block of land and as such the house its self is not considered of any real value, *(the assumption being that the buyer will demolish and develop the block)*. In such cases the cost of the land can make renovating the house financially unviable.

Vendor's terms and rent to buy:

"Vendor's terms" simply means that the Vendor will provide some, or all of the purchaser's finance for a nominated period of time. This is usually most attractive to buyers who do not have a deposit or a great credit rating as it offers them a means of purchasing a house where they otherwise would not be able to.

While it is not impossible it is unlikely you will find a seller willing to offer vendor's terms in a hot market, but it is not uncommon for property sales within families, such as between parents and children, the settling of a divorce or even between close associates to have some level of vendor's terms.

There are number of different ways vendor's terms can be offered. For example the vendor may agree to leave 10-20% of the value in the property for say five years *(to serve as a deposit for the buyer)*. The vendor will take a 2nd position mortgage over the property and the purchaser will pay the vendor interest on the 10-20% *(usually at a slightly higher rate than banks interest rate)*. At the end of the five-year period the purchaser will be required to pay the outstanding 10-20% *(either through savings or by refinancing)*.

If property values have increased over the five years the purchaser may find they have enough *equity** in the house to refinance without effecting their loan to value ratio.

Equity is the amount of a property's value that does not have a mortgage or lien over it. For example if you purchased a property with a 20% deposit you would be said to have 20% equity in the property.

In another example the vendor may offer *"rent to buy"* terms, whereby the prospective purchaser rents the property from the vendor at a higher than market rate, with an option to purchase after a nominated period. In such contracts it is usual for the vendor to subtract a portion of the rental paid against the purchase price should the prospective purchaser actually go ahead and purchase the property.

People purchasing on a rent to buy contract have the ability to make improvements to the property, thus increasing its value and hopefully putting themselves in an equity position that will enable them to get a mortgage.

There are literally thousands of permutations of vendor's terms contracts. And they can be written with any clauses, conditions and caveats as are agreeable to both buyer and seller.

NEGOTIATION

Most realtors are highly skilled negotiators. When negotiating with professional sales people it helps to know the tricks of the trade. If you are negotiating a private sale, there are a few do and don'ts you should bear in mind.

Do not tell the estate agent your budget, *(unless of course it is to tell them your bid has reached your absolute upper limit)*. Give them a budget range to work with, but keep a little in reserve.

Do not tell the real estate agent your circumstances. For example if you tell the agent your maximum budget, that you have sold your house and that you are in a hurry to buy, you have just provided them with knowledge they can use to get a better price out of you.

Don't act too keen. While it is impossible to act totally disinterested when buying a property *(after all if you weren't interested you wouldn't be making an offer)*, it is possible to give the agent the clear impression that you are only interested at a certain price and that there are other properties you are interested in. Let them know that if the price isn't right you could just as easily buy another property.

Be prepared to walk away and let them know that you are prepared to walk away.

I had a friend make an offer on a house that wasn't accepted. He desperately wanted the house but didn't want to pay more than he thought it was worth. He played it cool and walked away. Three weeks later the agent let him know the vendor was now prepared to accept the offer. It saved him $60k, which was the price of his renovation.

Remember estate agents and realtors only get paid when they

make a sale, so they will work both parties to make the sale happen. They will try to get buyers to up their offer and they will try to get sellers to drop the asking price. Whether buying or selling it is your job to make it clear to the agent that it will be much easier to get the other party to move on their price. If the agent knows you have more money or are desperate to purchase it is only logical to assume that you will be the one they will work the hardest.

Even in the US, where both the buyer and the seller have an agent acting on their behalf, the same principal applies. Your agent may technically be working for you, but primarily they will be working to make the sale happen so they can get paid. If they know they can squeeze more juice out of you to make the sale happen, they will.

While buyers in the USA usually have an agent acting on their behalf in many other places like the UK and Australia the buyer is usually totally on their own. In such places you can engage the services of a "buyers advocate" to help you negotiate, but unlike in the US (*where the seller usually "pays" for both their agent and the purchasers agent out of the proceeds of the sale*) it would be an extra expense on top of your purchase price.

When negotiating you should always bear in mind that price is not always what seals the deal. There are many things you can negotiate that can sweeten a deal and get it over the line. For example sometimes a seller will take a lesser offer if they can have a shorter settlement period and thus get their money earlier. Maybe they would take a 5% deposit if you agree to release the deposit before settlement? Maybe you will get a better price if you let the seller stay on and rent the place for 3 months after you settle? Maybe they simply want to know that you, as the new owner, will love and look after the garden they have spent 30 years creating.

I once bought a property from my next-door neighbour who did not want open inspections and needed the money from the sale to finish building his new house. He gave me a wonderful price and I let him stay on rent-free for 4 months after the sale so he could finish his build. It pays to ask.

SIGNING THE CONTRACT

NEVER sign a contract without having your closing agent *(solicitors/conveyancer)* review it. Get them to take you through it point by point to make sure you are absolutely clear on what you are signing. However if you are **100% sure** that the contract contains a cooling-off period, then you can sign it and use the cooling off period to get the contract thoroughly reviewed and explained.

If a property is being sold at auction it is quite normal for a prospective purchaser to request a copy of the contract well in advance of the auction date in order to have it looked over. If you have any particular conditions you want added to an auction contract you should discuss them with realtor or auctioneer well before the auction date.

Make sure all the details on the contract are correct and that the contract clearly states your chosen entity *(either you personally, or your company or trust)* as the purchaser.

Make sure that the contract contains all the terms and conditions you have agreed upon, and that the agreed sale price is clearly stated. Make sure the contract notes any deposit monies you have already paid *(and if and when any further deposit is due)*.

Note: If you intend to buy a property through a company or a trust it is important that you have that entity fully registered and legally in place before you sign the contracts.

*Even if you put a "**nominee clause**" in the contract, you may not be able to nominate an entity to step in as a the purchaser if that entity was not fully set up prior to your signing the contract, (and even if it is permitted in your jurisdiction, doing so can attract extra taxes and charges).*

(A "nominee clause" is a clause that allows the signatory to nominate another party to complete a purchase. For example, you would require such a clause if you were unable to attend an auction and sent someone else to bid and sign on your behalf).

PAYING THE DEPOSIT

It is quite common to give a small holding deposit *(often $500)*, upon agreeing on a sale before a contract goes unconditional; this is some times referred to as *"earnest money"*. This *"holding"* deposit is largely done as a gesture of good faith as it is usually fully refundable if the contract does not go ahead.

Once all the contract conditions are satisfied and the contract either goes to exchange or becomes unconditional the remainder of the deposit would usually be due. A deposit is most commonly 10%, however this is always up for negotiation.

Deposit Bonds: Many banks and financial institutions can provide you with a deposit bond or a deposit guarantee for a small fee. Instead of the buyer actually paying the deposit, a deposit bond acts like a guarantee for the vendor, that if the sale falls through they will pay the deposit on your behalf.

Most vendors are happy to take a deposit bond as it makes little difference to them, and it allows them to take offers from buyers who otherwise may not have deposit funds on hand to make an offer, *(for example, someone who has sold their house with an unconditional contract but has not yet settled and received the money).*

PART THREE

RENOVATING

PLANNING IT OUT

What type of renovation are you going to do? To some degree this will be determined by what you plan to do with the property afterwards. If you intend to keep it and rent it out then you may choose to do a quick superficial renovation, consisting of cleaning, painting, replacing blinds, curtains and floor coverings, and doing any necessary repairs. On the other hand if you are planning to sell then it may be worthwhile updating the kitchen and bathroom, maybe add another bathroom, do some landscaping etc. If you are working in an area where the prices can sustain it you may even wish to add an extension or a second story.

What ever you plan to do remember the golden rule of renovating:

"Do not overcapitalise".

Put simply what this means is don't spend too much money on the renovation. It is crucial when assessing what to do to a property that you get a clear idea of what the property will be worth after you have done it. Logically if adding an extension or another bathroom won't add more to the price of the property than it costs you to do, then you are *"overcapitalising"* and losing money.

When planning and budgeting a project I aim for a minimum 100% return on anything I spend. Say for example it cost me $10k to install a new kitchen; I would want that kitchen to add a minimum of $20k to the sale price of the property. When calculating how much value you need to add do not forget that you will also need to cover the costs of any structural repairs and any ancillary costs that may not actually add anything to the sale price. I personally wouldn't consider doing something that promised less than a 70% return on costs, *(unless of course it is a structural repair that is needed to make the house marketable).*

While certain things will always help push a property value up, *(like excellent storage space, an extra bedroom or off street parking)*, you should be careful about asking agents and realtors what improvements you ought to make to a property. Realtors' advice can be invaluable and they certainly know what attracts buyers, but most are not professional renovators and are not fully aware of the difficulties and expenses involved in certain upgrades. An Agent's advice can lead you to spending far more money than you need to if you are not careful.

I have known people to lose money on a house simply by unquestioningly following their agent's advice. For example an agent may tell you that people love bathrooms that are fully tiled from floor to ceiling. This may be true but if you are on a tight budget tiling floor to ceiling could double or triple the cost of your bathroom. The chances are that fewer well-chosen tiles and top notch decorating and dressing could be just as attractive to buyers. Once again, you need to have a look at recently sold properties in the area. Did they all have the recommended upgrades? Sometimes the desired item is more of a *"would like"*, than a *"must have"*.

Another example: a friend who is considering a two-story extension was recently advised by an agent that the extra wide walk way leading to his garden was something buyers would like. While this is undoubtedly true, it is a small house on a narrow block, and people would like extra living space inside considerably more.

Kerb appeal:

Never underestimate the value of kerb appeal. You should always set a budget for improving the kerb appeal of your property. Fresh paint, landscaping and a good fence will bring you some of the highest returns on your dollar spent. And don't forget the letterbox, street number and door-knocker.

Floor plans:

As a general rule, you don't need planning permission to alter the internal floor plan of property, *(unless it is heritage listed)*. If you are planning a mid level renovation it can be worth looking at the floor plan to see if you can do more with the space. Extra bedrooms *(as long as they are not too small)* and a second bathroom will always add money.

People love a separate laundry *(or utility room)*, but in many places *(such as the UK)* this is by no means essential for a low to mid range property. In some places the laundry has as view over the garden, whereas many people would prefer it if you installed a European laundry *(a laundry that is in a cupboard off a hallway)*, and knocked out the wall to incorporate the garden view into the kitchen/ dining /family rooms.

The cost of altering the floor plan will depend largely on the structure. Timber framed houses with stud walls are relatively inexpensive to alter, where as brick or masonry walls can cost significantly more to move. When removing walls you will most often have to add structural support to the opening, *(either a timber or steel beam)*. This should not be done without professional advice.

Removing fireplaces can add extra space and give more flexibility to a floor plan so it is worth considering. Removing a fireplace does not necessarily mean you have to remove the chimney, as often you can remove the fireplace under the ceiling line, and add a structural support lintel in the roof cavity to take the weight of the remaining brick work. This can save you the expense of having to patch the hole in the roof from where a chimney was removed. It can allow you to remove a fireplace from a terraced or semi-detached property where the chimney is shared with the neighbouring property, or even remove a fireplace where the roof line is protected by some kind of heritage overlay.

When redesigning your floor plan you should think about the effect any changes may have on the light and the views. Anything you can do to add light and long vistas is generally money well spent. For example sometimes I like to use glass doors at the end of hallways. Hallways are often dark and a glass door opening into a bright living space not only brings light into the hallway it can give the impression of more space and sometimes even provide garden glimpses from the front door.

Think about heating, air conditioning and noise. Stairs leading up from an open plan living room are very fashionable but they can be a nightmare to live with. Heat and noise will rise up into the stairwell making the whole house noisy, and difficult and expensive to heat or cool.

Give some thought to separating your zones. If you can create separate living and sleeping zones this can add greatly to the amenity of the home and save you money in utility costs. To this end it is always better to avoid having bathrooms and bedrooms that enter directly off a living area.

If you have a toilet or bathroom that has a door to a living area try and find a way to change that. People do not like using a powder room that opens up to a living area and it will repel many buyers.

The following is an example of a floor plan that was amended to great effect. In this property we expanded the size of the master bedroom, added a full wall of storage and an en-suite.

We also moved the bathroom and laundry closer to the bedrooms, allowing us to make a huge open plan kitchen/dinning/living area that overlooked the deck and the garden. We also separated the space into a living zone and a bedroom zone, which added to the privacy and amenity of the home.

As you can see there was a lot of wasted space in the original floor plan. By reconfiguring the floor space we managed to turn that large unusable hallway at the back of the house into valuable living area. You will also notice we moved the door to the rear bedroom, so you enter from the hallway, and not directly from the living space. It is not always possible to do this, but if you can it will always be an improvement.

SETTING YOUR BUDGET

Time frames often don't permit thorough quoting before purchase, so costing out your first few projects can be difficult and there is often a certain amount of guesswork involved. But once you have purchased and are committed to the project you can really start to nail down your budget.

At this stage it is crucial that you again remember the golden rule...

"Do not overcapitalise"

The first thing you need to do is establish exactly how much money you have and how much money you can safely spend on a project. If you haven't already done it take a look at similar sales in the area and find out the maximum sale price previously achieved in your street. You need to know up front how your property will compare with those properties once you have finished the renovation.

Taking all other costs into account you need to make sure your renovation spend doesn't take you over the price ceiling for your type of property in your area and that there is enough of a profit margin for it to be worth your time.

For example: If you bought a three bedroom one bathroom house for £200k, and the average price for a renovated 3 bed 1 bath house in that street is £310k. You have holding and associated costs of £20k, and plan to spend a maximum of £60k on the renovation. In this scenario you could reasonably expect to make £30k profit, whereas if you spent £85k on the renovation, would only made £5k.

If however the average price of four bed two bathroom house was £410k that might have a bearing on your plans. You might be better to spend an extra £30k and add an extension.

Once you have established how much you can comfortably afford to spend, you need to plan out what to do with that money. I find it very helpful to prioritise my spending, and a table like the one on the following page can be very helpful.

Must Have	Should Have	Could Have
Roof Repair - fix leaks	Changes to floor plan	Spa bath
Re stumping	En-suite	External deck & pagoda
Rewiring & new light fittings	Front fence	New doors and mouldings
New bathroom	New kitchen	New polished floor boards
Fresh paint	Landscaping	Gas log fire
New carpet & curtains	Built in robes	Granite counter tops
Double glazing	Decorative plaster work	Floor to ceiling tiles
Central heating	New door furniture	A conservatory

Many people who are new to renovating make the mistake of becoming emotionally attached to items that really belong in the *"could have"* column. Instead of taking care of the important items they spend their money on bling things, only to find that the house comes up lacking when a buyer gets a building report done.

While the latest bling things can undoubtedly add to your sale price buyers usually recognise lipstick on a pig. If you haven't fixed the basic structural issues buyers will not be impressed. Fixing the fundamentals, doing a more basic renovation and choosing the right way to dress your house for sale can often have a much bigger impact on the final selling price than installing the latest flashy thing.

A word of warning on budgeting:

It is absolutely essential that you make sure you have the funds available to do what it is you have planned. Nothing will get you in more trouble than running out of money half way through a renovation. If you are forced to sell a house that has been half renovated it is almost guaranteed you will loose money.

If however you are buying a house that is half renovated then you may well score a bargain. When planning your project it is better to plan to do something you know you can afford, that will make you a modest profit, rather than attempt something that might stretch you too far and end in a forced sale.

Rubbish removal:

Rubbish removal is the one expense that most beginners overlook. And it can be very expensive, particularly if you have to remove hazardous waste like asbestos. Depending on where you are and how much you are stripping out, tip fees and bin hire can cost you thousands. Get quotes and know your approximate costs before you start.

PLANS AND PERMITS

Generally there are two stages to getting plans and permits to build or extend. The planning permit and the building permit.

Planning permits:

The planning stage involves getting your plans drawn up and submitted to your local authority to see if they will approve your proposal. While there are some exceptions*, as a general rule all extensions, second story additions and new builds require planning permission. This not a process for the feint hearted.

In the UK for example they allow some small extensions and conservatories to be built without planning permission. In parts of Australia you can build a house without planning permission if the block is a certain size and the design complies with the relevant building code - but you need to take professional advice on this.

At the planning stage you will have to choose between using an architect or draftsperson. If you are working on your own home or you want to do something dazzlingly original you may be better off with an architect. If however you are working on a low to mid range property I would recommend using a draftsperson.

Architects not only cost a lot more for their services, they very rarely consider budget in their designs. If you are working to a budget be very clear about it with who ever is doing your drawings. Little things, like requesting that they specify standard sized windows can save you thousands in window treatments as you will be able to buy binds, curtains and shutters off the shelf.

Discuss your materials preferences with your draftsperson, things like what exterior cladding you use or whether to use timber, UPVC or metal windows can have a huge bearing on your costs. For example if you have a blind wall that cannot readily be seen do you really need to clad it in brick? Do you need to clad the 2nd story in brick?

Once you have had plans drawn up, a process that usually takes at least 6-8 weeks, it can take anything from 6 weeks to 12 months to obtain planning permission, depending on your local authority. Some local authorities have onerous heritage restrictions and some are just plain slow.

In the case of one guy I know it took him four years to get his plans through simply because he got involved in a fight with the local authority. As they didn't like him they used every legal means they could to stall him, *(so make sure you are always polite when dealing with your local planning authority).*

Human nature being what it is, no matter what you submit you will almost always be asked to make some amendment or other, *(even if you have had pre submission meetings and have done exactly what they have suggested).* I often put some small but obvious error in the plans that I know will not be approved. This gives the planners something to take issue with, and most often it stops them picking apart my plans any further.

For example in a recent submission for a roof garden I put a low fence that overlooked the neighbour's garden on the original plans. As this was not to code they picked up on it instantly and demanded I change it. Even though my proposal was without precedent in the area this was the only change I had to make.

Building or Construction Permits:

Once you have your planning permission you can then move on to the second stage, the building or construction permits. In many places a building permit must be taken out by a registered builder, although there is usually some form of *"owner builder"* permit available to people who wish to manage work being done on their own homes. You will need to check with your local authority to find out the application rules in your area.

Building or construction permits are also known as Building Regulations Approval in the UK.

In order to get a building permit you will usually need to get soil tests, engineering and working drawings done. These drawings show your builder and the building inspector/surveyor what the exact measurements of your building are, what materials are being used, and what methods and building codes apply to each aspect of the build. They will detail where all the plumbing and storm water connections are and where all the lighting and electrical points are. In some areas you may need to get an energy rating certificate and landscape plans done as well.

It can take several weeks, *(and sometimes months if your planner or engineer is slow)* to get these drawings done, and once they are complete they will usually need to be reviewed and approved by a building inspector/surveyor before a building permit is issued.

If you are thinking of doing an extension that requires planning permission make sure you factor in a long holding period.

ENERGY EFFICIENCY

From an ethical standpoint I believe in doing everything your budget permits to reduce the environmental footprint of a house. The way I see it we owe it to future generations not to squander their inheritance.

Some markets will pay a premium for energy efficient features like top-level insulation, solar panels, double-glazing and low-e glass, while others will not. Generally the less expensive the area, the less likely you are to get a return on money spent on energy efficiency. In some markets, such as the UK, people expect double-glazing and unless you are renovating a heritage property *(where changing the windows is not possible)* failing to provide it could make your house difficult to sell.

HIRING BUILDERS AND TRADES PEOPLE

There are two main ways you can engage people to work on your house. The first is to engage a contractor or builder, the other is to act as your own contractor and engage the individual trades yourself.

Some jurisdictions have laws stating that you must engage a licensed builder/contractor to undertake works of a certain value or magnitude, so check with your local authority as to the laws in your state or county.

Contracting a builder:

A builder will usually provide you with a fixed price contract for a detailed schedule of works. The time frame, payment schedule, any penalties for delays and any provision the builder makes for *unforeseen expenses** would usually form part of this contract.

(Example, you may be putting in a new concrete slab for an extension. When you start excavating you discover there are rocks in the soil that need to be removed. This is an expense that could not have been accurately foreseen, so often a builder will make an allowance in the contract to charge the cost of removing any rocks, should it be necessary).

If you are entering a fixed price contract be very clear on exactly what is included in the price and what the potential unforeseen expenses are. Make sure **everything** is clearly itemised in the contract schedule.

In most fixed price contracts the builder will purchase all the materials and hire the individual trades needed to complete the job, although like anything in renovations, this is up for negotiation.

Fixtures and fittings will be specified in the contract so be sure to be thorough in detailing exactly what you want. You may want to choose and purchase your own fixtures and fittings, such as tiles, kitchen cabinets, baths, tap ware, light fittings etc., and provision for this can usually be made in the contract. In such cases the builder will usually allocate a sum of money that is set aside to cover the price of that item and that amount is taken back against the invoice.

For example: Say you don't like the choice of tiles the builder is offering and you want to buy your own. The contract may specify that the builder has allowed $20 per square meter for tiles. In which case if you bought 15 square meters of tiles, the builder would take $300 off the final contract price.

For a beginner, or someone simply renovating their own home engaging a builder can be a less stressful option, as they take care of everything; but it is not without risks. When engaging a builder on a fixed price contract you are bound to that builder. If you are not happy with the standard or progress of their work it can be difficult to get out of the contract and engage someone else. Many times such disputes end up in court costing you precious time and money.

When you are thinking of hiring a builder make sure you get verifiable references, check their insurance and check that they are registered with the local professional builders association. While most builders are reputable there are cowboys out there and you need to be careful. Some so called builders have been known to stand over clients and demand money up front for materials and then disappear without doing any work. It is better to pay a little more and go with an established builder with a good local reputation than to risk your hard earned money on an unknown with a fabulous quote and a great sales pitch.

NOTE: Once you have engaged a builder on contract try to avoid making any changes to your plans as builders will often charge an exorbitant premium on any alterations to the plans or contract.

Contracting individual trades:

If you are hiring your own individual trades people you can either get them to quote out the whole of their particular job, or pay them by the hour.

A fixed quote and contract will give you more certainty over your budget, but be aware many trades people will factor in a bit extra in case they run into problems. You also run many of the same risks that you have with contracting a builder. If you are unhappy with their work it can be harder to sack them and doing so may leave you open to litigation.

If you hire by the hour there is the risk that they will *"go slow"*. However if you are going to be on site with them this is much less of a problem. If you contract trades on an hourly basis it is a very simply matter to get rid of a tradesperson who is under performing. You will also avoid paying a hefty premium on any changes you make to your plans.

I generally prefer to hire hourly for carpentry plumbing and electrical work, as it leaves me with a lot more freedom and flexibility to make changes and it gives me much greater control over the project. For any roofing, plastering, painting, floor sanding, tiling, brickwork, re-stumping or underpinning I prefer to get an upfront quote.

SCHEDULING

If you are hiring a builder scheduling trades and contractors will be taken care of for you. However if you are engaging individual trades you will need to make sure that you have booked the right trade for each task, and that everyone arrives in in the right order.

Remember that when doing a renovation time is money so it is important to keep your schedule moving. Do not wait until you need a trade to call them and book them in. Trades people are very rarely available on the day you call so try to give them as much notice as you can. If you have them booked in and then find you are delayed for a day or two they can often switch your job with another client. As long as your job is on their roster its usually not too long before they can slot your job back in.

If you are hiring individual trades your carpenter will be your mainstay tradesperson who will be with you from the start of the job right through to the end. Your carpenter will know better than anyone where you are up to so keep the lines of communication open. Ask how long they see each task taking, ask them what materials they will need for the next few days and make sure they are ordered and delivered in good time.

1. Disconnection

You can't safely pull out walls or kitchens or bathrooms with the utilities still connected, so day one you need to disconnect any effected plumbing and electrical wires.

Trades Needed: Electrician, Plumber

2. Demolition and strip out

The strip out would usually be done by you, your carpenter and or labourers. While pulling out old cupboards and carpets doesn't require a lot of skill you should always check with a professional as to whether any walls you plan to remove are structural or load bearing. Make sure you have at least one qualified building professional on site when removing any walls and make sure you have adequate props on site to support the structure until any required beams or lintels are installed.

Trades Needed: Carpenter, labourers

3. Structural repairs - foundations/damp course etc.

Most often you would strip out before fixing the foundations but depending on the property you may decide to fix the foundations first. This would usually only be done if the property is on stumps and were high enough off the ground for re-stumpers to get in underneath the building. If they need to pull up the flooring you will have to strip out first.

NOTE: If you are installing a concrete slab as a replacement foundation and floor or as part of an extension you will need to "rough in" any electrical work and plumbing that need to run under the slab BEFORE you lay any concrete, (see step 6).

Trades Needed: Carpenter (for repairing the odd stump), underpinning, re-stumping, concreter

4. New framing, windows, baths and shower bases installed

This would include any structural repairs to the frame and roof trusses, installing any new walls windows or skylights, setting the bath and shower bases and framing up any built in robes.

Trades Needed: Carpenter

5. Roof, gutters and flashing

Depending on your roof structure your carpenter may be able to make small repairs to your roof or gutters, but you would need to discuss this to find out whether it is something your carpenter would be able to undertake. If not you will need to get a specialised roofing contractor or roof plumber. *(A roof plumber is someone who specialises in gutters and drainage).*

Trades Needed: Carpenter, roofer or roof plumber

5. Exterior cladding

This step can happen along side any roof repair, although generally you will need to have all the exterior cladding in place before any gutters and down pipes are installed.

Trades Needed: Carpenter, bricklayer, renderer, *(depending on the type of external cladding)*

6. Rough in

Once the frame is complete you need to get your electrician and plumber back to install electrical cabling, water pipes and drainage that are required. If your plumber is not doing your central heating you will need to get the heating people in at this stage as well. Make sure to include any wiring required for doorbells, CTV cameras, ceiling fans, and thermostats.

You will need to have selected your taps, or know for certain what type of taps you intend to use before the plumber roughs in your bathroom. Different types of taps require different plumbing configurations so this is a decision you need to make early.

NOTE: If you are using wall mounted taps your plumber will need to know what thickness of tile you are using and the thickness of the wall cladding (such as plaster board or cement sheet etc.), as this will determine how far back into the frame the tap mounts are set. It is crucial you discuss this with your plumber, as they will not always ask. If they set the taps at the wrong depth your taps may not fit. It can be very difficult, messy and expensive to adjust this later so make sure you get it right at rough in.

If however you do find your self with this problem you can buy spindle extenders (although they will not work with all taps as they tend to be bulky), and there are some taps on the market with reversible flanges that can be set back over quite a wide range of depths, and this may save you from having to rip out your tiling to reset your taps.

Trades Needed: Electrician, plumber, ducted heating and air,

7. New flooring

Lay any structural flooring that is needed, whether it is floorboards, compressed concrete sheets *(for bathrooms and wet areas under tiles)* or particleboard flooring *(for under carpet or floating floors)*. The one exception to this would be in the bathroom, where the plumber may need to lift the floor sheets at a later date to connect pipe work. In such cases it is best to cut the flooring to size and leave it in place until the plumber has finished making his all connections before screwing it down.

Trades Needed: Carpenter

8. Plaster work

I recommend getting a professional plasterer as a poor wall or ceiling finish will always compromise your sale price. Professional plasterers are usually very quick, where as people attempting their own plasterwork tend to be very very slow, which can delay the project. Ending up with a poor finish and lost time make doing your own plastering a false economy.

Trades Needed: Plasterer

9. Install laundry and kitchen cupboards, countertops, and fit off any built in Robes

At this point the carpenter *(and stonemason if your are using stone countertops)* would install any kitchen and laundry cupboards and sinks, and install the shelves and hanging rails to any fitted robes.

Trades Needed: Carpenter, Kitchen Installer, Stonemason

10. Install doorframes, doors, architraves and skirting

Trades Needed: Carpenter

11. Waterproofing, tiling and splash backs

Your tiler will usually be able to do any waterproofing required and this would usually be included in the quote. If you are using glass splash backs or shower walls they would be installed at this stage.

Trades Needed: Tiler and or glazier, (or carpenter if you are installing stainless steel splash backs)

12. Painting

Trades Needed: Painter

13. Electrical and plumbing fit offs

The electrician returns to install all the light fittings and power outlets and the plumber comes back to install the taps and connect the drainage to all the sinks, baths, showers and basins.

Trades Needed: Electrician and Plumber

14. Polish floor boards

Trades Needed: Floor sander

15. Floating floors and vinyl

Floating floors, vinyl or carpet should be installed after polishing any floorboards to avoid the risk of scuffing or contaminating the carpet with dust.

16. Laying carpet

Carpet should always be the last flooring to be laid. Always have your carpet professionally laid, as this is not something you can do yourself to a satisfactory standard.

Trades needed: Carpet layer

17. Window Dressings

Window dressings can be a do it yourself item, with standard off the shelf products, or for more expensive properties you may want to get them made up bespoke and installed professionally.

Trades needed: DIY or carpenter for off the shelf option, Blind or curtain company for bespoke options.

DYI OR PROFESSIONAL TRADES PEOPLE?

Renovators are always trying to save money, and one of most common ways of trimming the budget is to do some of the work yourself. When planning out your job and working out what you can and can't do yourself it pays to remember that time is money.

In most cases professionals will get things done a lot faster than you can. Remember that for every day that you hold your property empty you are paying mortgage, council taxes, water rates and utilities etc.

You should also factor in the cost of your own labour. If you were working at a job what would you be earning?

The time of year can also be a factor, is winter approaching? Do you need to get the project finished and on the market while the weather is still good?

Apart from the obvious trades like electrics, gas fitting and plumbing where you clearly need to employ registered trades people, there are some other jobs that I think you should always have done by a professional. Unless you have a lot of experience I would not consider doing my own carpentry, tiling, floor sanding, skim coats or hard plastering *(dry-walling can be OK to do DIY but I would practice taping and seaming on off cuts first)*. Often times doing these things yourself does not actually save you money, and if you are inexperienced the finish you could expect to get may not be up to standard.

When working out which jobs you should DIY people often underestimate the amount of time it takes to properly manage a successful project. You need to be constantly trouble shooting, amending schedules, sourcing materials, paying bills, arranging deliveries, liaising with neighbours, building inspectors and local authorities and organising rubbish removal etc. Many professional renovators spend a lot more time on the phone, *(or running off to get that bit of timber or box of screws the carpenter needs)* than they do on the tools.

BARGAIN HUNTING

Fixtures and fittings: Fixtures and fittings are without doubt one the major costs of any renovation. Anything you can do bring down the cost of such items will ultimately add profit to your bottom-line so don't be afraid to look outside the main street stores. You can quite literally save tens of thousands of dollars if you are prepared to put in the time hunting for bargains.

There are many different places you can hunt for bargains, such as scratch and dent bulk stores, auction yards, excess stock sales, trades warehouses, demolition yards, ex display sales and even Ebay. Ask around in your area, search the net and find out what is available in your locale, you may be pleasantly surprised.

Ebay is an excellent place to source building materials. I have bought everything from floorboards, doors, windows, light fittings, toilets, sinks, taps, 2nd hand kitchens, new kitchens, dishwashers, decking boards, air conditioners, curtains and cushions to garden furniture for cents in the dollar.

I have also bought many bargain items due to a misspelled or inappropriate listing. There are a few web sites such as fatfingers.com that will search for items that have been listed on ebay with spelling mistakes. You would be surprised what bargains can be had.

I also make a habit of always looking at seller's other items. I have found many amazing bargains that were badly listed that way. For example I once bought a near new top of the line 2nd hand kitchen with all near new appliances *(cooktop, oven, dishwasher, range hood, sink, tap ware)* that was listed as *"white goods"*. As no one who was looking for a kitchen or a cooktop or dishwasher would do a search for *"white goods"* there was only one other bidder and I ended up buying the lot for $80. Just the other day I bought 2 brand new double glazed UPVC windows for $50 that were incorrectly listed as "pvc widows", which was incredible score as the retail price of those two windows is approximately $3000, *(and a couple of similar windows I was "watching" had just sold for $600 each).*

When shopping for bargains on eBay it pays to use an automated bidder such as auctionsniper.com It is an inexpensive service and can save you from having to hover over the computer to bid when they are finishing. While it doesn't guarantee you will win every auction it will certainly up your average. And it will stop you bidding up the price unnecessarily.

TIP: Shop wisely! Cheaper is not always better. I know a guy who has a thing for getting bargain fixtures and fittings. He will, for example, buy a wonderful luxury bath at auction for a bargain price and then spend weeks modifying his bathroom, moving walls and windows etc., to try and fit it in. In the end it costs him three or four times more than if he had bought the right sized bath and paid full retail for it. Something is only a bargain if you can use it. If it is not fit for your purpose then it is just a waste of your time and money.

DOORS AND WINDOWS

There are many different types of doors and windows you can choose from and there are many factors that can influence what choices you make, such as the weather, energy efficiency, sound insulation, available space, aesthetics and of course price.

What doors and windows you ultimately choose will depend on your circumstances, but there are a few guiding principals to bear in mind.

Be consistent: Pick a style and run with it. If you are using 4 panel doors don't just throw in a couple of 6 panel doors because you bought them cheap and had them lying around. Being consistent will give your renovation a more cohesive, designer feel and that usually means a better sale price. You can of course use a combination of solid and glass doors, but try to choose just one style for your solid doors and one style for your glass doors.

Where windows are concerned, you can alter the type of windows from room to room *(eg: awning, double hung),* but I would try to maintain some consistency in the style, particularly on the front and rear face of the building. I would not, for example, use colonial bars in one room, and plain glass in the next.

External (entry) Doors:

Exterior doors are generally stronger in construction than

internal doors, so make sure any door you buy for external use is designed and manufactured to withstand the weather and will meet your security needs.

There are many different types and styles of entry doors including double doors, side light and entry door, French (glass) doors, sliding doors, stacker doors, bi-fold doors, security doors, fly screen doors etc., and they can be made of anything from timber, to upvc, glass, aluminium or even steel.

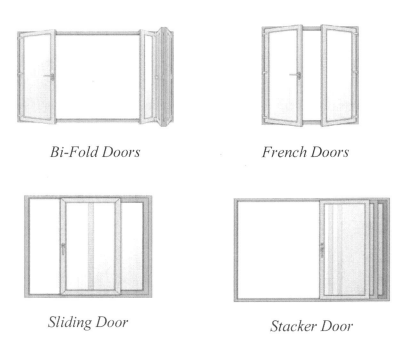

Bi-Fold Doors   *French Doors*

Sliding Door   *Stacker Door*

In areas where back gardens are privacy fenced, glass doors leading out to a deck, garden or patio will always attract a premium. Bi-fold and French doors are currently the popular choices, however if you only have a small courtyard or limited garden space I would consider going for a sliding or stacking door. Bi-folds and French doors usually require at least a meter/yard clearance to open and this will eat into your precious outdoor space, where as you could easily put a cafe table next to the non opening side of slider or stacker door.

Many types of exterior doors, such as aluminium or UPVC will come from the manufacturer with locks already fitted, but with timber doors you generally have to supply and fit your own, so don't forget to budget extra for locks if you need to.

While deadbolt and deadlocks are fairly straight forward for DIYer's to fit, mortise locks are tricky and surprisingly time consuming to install. Most of the better quality designer entry handles are made for mortise locks, but you will usually require a professional carpenter to install one.

Mortise lock   *Dead bolt*

Internal doors:

When assessing what doors to use internally you need to weigh up how your choice will affect your sale price. There are many cheap, "hollow core" doors on the market and while they may be perfectly suitable for a home in a less expensive price range *(or a rental property)*, using them in an upmarket renovation could cost you big money on your sale price.

Solid doors are comparatively expensive, but they add a lot to the feel of quality of the home. You can buy some lovely veneer doors, *(if you are going for a timber look)* that look stunning and have the weight of a solid door but are considerably cheaper. If you plan to paint your doors there are also some fabulous paint grade timber or composite board doors available that are reasonably priced and have the weight and feel of solid timber.

In some mid range houses where the budget is tight I have used a combination of solid and hollow doors; using solid doors for the living areas and anywhere you might expect guests to be, and using hollow core doors for the laundry, en-suite and maybe some of the ancillary bedrooms. But as always, you need to weigh it up as to what is appropriate for your project.

When fitting new doors, and doorjambs *(a door jamb is the timber frame the door hangs on),* take note of the weight of the door. If you are hanging a solid door always use a solid timber jamb. There are many cheaper composite board and MDF jambs on the market *(that are made of glued compressed wood chips and saw dust)* that are suitable for hollow doors but may not take the weight of a solid door. This can lead to the door dropping and the screw holes routing out and disintegrating. This is difficult to repair and you will most likely have to replace the jamb. If however your wall is timber framed you may be able to hang a solid door on a composite jambs by using longer screws, and screwing through the jamb and into the timber frame behind.

Sliding doors can be great space savers. Most sliders are hung from a track above the doorway, although in some places you can buy cavity units that fit into a stud wall which allows the door to recesses back into the wall *(for some reason these units are not broadly available in the UK)*. Sliding doors do not generally give the same level of privacy, noise and temperature insulation as a hung door, so they are not usually a first choice. That said, recently some architects have been designing extra large Japanese style sliding door/walls, that seal off parts of large open plan spaces which can give a stunning effect and add enormous flexibility to a larger space.

Door Furniture and Hardware:

It is worth spending a little extra on your door furniture. As a buyer moves through your house the door handles are the one thing they are guaranteed to touch; if they feel cheap and shoddy it will create a very negative impression. However if your buyer feels the weight of a good solid door handle it will give the impression of quality, *(even if your doors are cheap).*

Windows:

There are many types and styles of windows, including fixed, double hung, casement, sliders, awning, tilt and turn, bi-fold, hopper, bay, bow and garden windows. What you will have in your property will depend largely on where you are located and the age and style of the property.

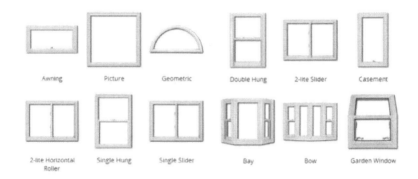

You may choose to repair or replace some or all of the windows in a property, but if you are replacing any windows **make sure the replacements fit.** This may sound obvious but I have seen countless expensive windows for sale on eBay because someone ordered the wrong size.

When retrofitting in brick it is always better to order slightly smaller, *(by say 2-3cm or 1-1/2 inches and then cover the gap)*, than to order your widow oversized. Be aware when measuring that your hole may not be plumb. If you only measure one side there is a chance the other side may be a bit smaller, so measure all four sides and check it with a spirit level. However if you are installing new double glazed windows in a brick house you would generally get your window company in to do the measure-up for you.

If you are working on a timber house then going slightly bigger is not usually a problem, as it is fairly easy to cut a hole a bit larger. This can allow you to shop for second hand windows, and possibly pick up some wonderful period feature windows that can really add to the "Wow! Factor".

In the property above we replaced the ugly old aluminium front windows with beautiful period lead light windows we got on eBay, which gave a wonderful lift to the property both inside and out. We also installed a period lead light window in the ultra modern kitchen to great effect.

Repair or replace?

If you have some beautiful old windows that are not opening properly or are showing signs of rot you may want to repair them. Depending on how far gone they are this can be well worth doing or an expensive waste of time. Minor rot, broken sash chords *(a sash cord is the rope that holds the weights in old double hung windows)* and minor sticking can be easily dealt with, but trying to fix windows with structural rot, crumbling sashes, or broken dowel or mortise and tenon joints can eat up days of your time and often still look pretty average when you are done.

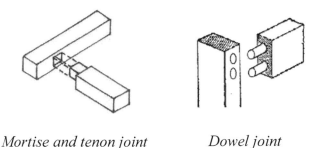

Mortise and tenon joint   *Dowel joint*

If you have a particularly lovely lead light in a rotten sash, or a beautiful bay window with only one or two sashes that are badly damaged *(due to gutter issues for instance)* sometimes your best and cheapest option is to get replacement sashes made and have any lead light refitted.

In assessing whether it is worth spending hours repairing a window you need to factor in your hourly wage against the cost of replacement.

KITCHENS

It is a well known fact in real estate: kitchens and bathrooms sell houses. Get the kitchen right and you are half way there, get it wrong and many buyers will reject the house outright, no matter how much they like the rest of the property. The kitchen is the heart of the home and it needs to be not only aesthetically pleasing but also highly functional.

When you are planning your kitchen always try to maximise your bench and storage space. Insufficient work surfaces and storage space are the most common complaints buyers have when viewing kitchens. Imagine your self living and working in the kitchen. Can you reach everything easily? You may be six feet tall, but most women are not. Is it possible for someone to make a cup of tea or get a drink from the fridge while someone else is cooking? If not you may find your kitchen just won't click with buyers.

When installing a new kitchen there are a myriad of choices to be made. Every option has its pluses and minuses, and you need to bear this in mind as you make your choices.

Cabinets:

While it can be tempting to rip out your cabinets and replace them, however if your cabinets are still in good order it may be cheaper and just as effective to get new doors made.

When considering the style and colour of your kitchen it is important to take the light level into account, as a dark kitchen will feel much smaller.

While they have been fashionable in recent times dark cabinets can really suck the light out of a room, whereas highly reflective gloss white cabinets can increase the light level 2 to 3 times. Kitchens that feel small and dark are definite buyer turn offs, so unless you have a lot of natural light and space I would avoid dark cabinetry.

The above kitchen was a low budget refit in a small dark space that didn't have a lot of natural light. We used white gloss cabinets and added the window at the side to bring extra light into the room. We made the fridge accessible by others when someone is cooking. We used a combination of down-lights and pendant lighting, to give a choice of lighting, and we used a drop in sink to give the designer effect, (but without the added expense of polishing the stone edges for a high end under bench option).

As there was not a lot of cupboard space we chose to go for a telescopic range hood, *(rather than a canopy),* to allow for a little extra storage; and we used a built in cooktop and oven *(as they are well liked and a more affordable option)*. For the splash back we used large polished porcelain tiles, to give that glass look for a lot less money. And of course, to dress the cheap cabinets we used heavy weight designer stainless steel handles.

Counter tops:

There are a huge variety of countertops to choose from, each with their own advantages and disadvantages.

Timber:

Timber looks beautiful, it is warm, natural, easy to install and transport and people like it. On the down side timber scores and burns fairly easily, and you will need to seal it well or it will rot and blacken where it is subject to moisture. *(I recommend several coats of marine estapol, then sand back with fine steel wool, wax and polish).* I would not use timber for a property you intend to rent out.

Granite:

Granite is hard wearing, durable, scratch and burn resistant. It is expensive to buy, transport and install and there are a limited range of colour options. If using granite I would lean toward something neutral in tone, like a grey or a black as it will endure better through changes in fashion.

Quartz Stone:

Made from reconstituted quartz and stone, quartz stone is a mid to higher priced option that comes in a wide range of colours. While slightly more prone to staining and chipping than granite it is none the less quite durable. Quartz stone is low maintenance and easy to care for and most stains can be removed with bathroom bleach.

Laminate Formica:

Laminate and Formica are inexpensive, easy to clean, durable and come in a practically unlimited range of patters, colours and textures. You can get a number of different profiles including hard square edged, round roll edged, square rolled edge. They don't score, burn and stain easily and can be a great quick easy option for a rental or a low to mid end property.

Tile:

Tile counter tops are extremely popular and widely used in the USA, but I am not a fan. They are prone to chipping and cracking, and are difficult to keep clean as the grout attracts dirt and grease, Tile counter tops require regular hard scrubbing to keep them sanitary and they have been known to have jagged edges that can catch on things if they are not extremely well laid.

Stainless Steel:

For fans of the commercial industrial look you cannot go past stainless steel counter tops. They are highly durable, easy to clean, not prohibitively expensive and will give your renovation that urban chic factor.

Splash backs:

Splash-backs *(or back splashes)* are usually tile, glass or stainless steel. Glass is expensive, but gives a wonderful look. I have given kitchens a glass look for one quarter of the price using large by polished porcelain tiles.

Stainless steel is common for behind cookers and gives an easy clean, grout free surface for any grease or cooking splashes. Tiles are the most common splash back as they are inexpensive, practical and generally look good. I would however avoid the checkerboard of bright colours that is often seen in the UK, as it can be a real turn off for some buyers. Stick with one colour for your splash back tiles.

I would also avoid mosaic tiles, particularly behind a cook top as they don't tend to wear well. Due to their small size mosaic tiles have a higher percentage of surface grout, which can easily attract grease and stains.

Sinks:

With so many different types of sinks available your bog standard stainless steel sink is far from your only option. White porcelain butlers sinks, moulded Corian sinks, granite composite sinks, sinks with draining boards, sinks without draining boards, top-mount (drop in) sinks, under-mount sinks, there is a choice for every taste and budget.

The cost of sinks can vary a lot, but just because you are watching your budget doesn't mean you can't have something that looks high end. If you are on a budget you may choose to go for a top mount sink without a draining board, or a white ceramic sink, both of which can look stunningly high-end but aren't necessarily expensive to purchase or install.

Ovens and cook tops:

The first choice you have to make is gas or electric. While most people do not have a strong preference when it comes to ovens, many people prefer gas cooktops, and as such I would always install a gas cook top if gas supply were available in the area.

In areas where only bottled gas is available the choice is a little more nuanced. While some people will prefer gas even if they have to go to the trouble of ordering gas bottle refills, others will not like having to refill bottled gas at all. In such circumstances I would probably go with an induction cooktop. Induction cooktops have only been around for a few years but they have already made their mark as a high-end desirable item. While not quite as good to cook with as gas they are much better than the older model electric cook tops. They have far better temperature control and are also much safer around children as they instantly turn off when you remove the pan from the hotplate.

Built in or freestanding? Freestanding cookers are usually more expensive but you will not have to buy a cabinet to put them in or have your counter tops cut out in order to install the cooktop. Mostly this decision will come down to a matter of taste.

Electric cooktops and ovens draw a huge amount of current and will need to run on their own high amp electrical circuit. Do not forget this when you are at rough-in stage, if you are installing an electric cooktop or oven for the first time or in a new location your electrician will need to run a separate high amp line back to the circuit board especially for your cooker. Many cookers are dual fuel, with gas cook top and electric oven, do not assume that because a cooker has a gas cooktop the oven is also gas. Check and make sure you are installing the required services.

Range hoods:

A range hood is an essential item in a modern kitchen. Venting range hoods are always preferable as they extract all cooking odours steam and grease to the outside, leaving the air in your kitchen clean and fresh. If however you have a terraced property or are unable to access an exterior wall a good quality recirculated range hood will still effectively extract the grease and condense the steam. With any range hood make sure you wash the filters regularly to keep them in good working order to avoid the build up of stale cooking odours.

There are a few considerations when choosing a range hood, for example do you choose a telescopic or canopy hood? While canopy hoods are very popular at the moment, if you are short on cupboard space, or if you are going for a more streamlined look you might choose to go with telescopic *(or slide out)* range hood. Another consideration is how loud is it? I recently installed a fabulous looking canopy hood only to find it made the noise of a small airport. I actually ended up replacing it because it was simply too loud. The noise level of a unit is usually noted in the specifications under "Db's". Be sure to check this out and look for a unit with the lowest possible noise level, preferably under 40Db.

BATHROOMS

More often than not adding a second bathroom will return a premium in a family home. If you can attach an en-suite to the master bedroom it is always going to add value. As with the kitchen, imagine yourself using the space. Can you reach everything easily? Is there enough room to bend over and dry your toes?

Whether you are doing a cheap renovation or tackling a top end property the main issue with bathrooms is functionality. You need to have enough space to undress and dry yourself without tripping over, or banging and bruising yourself on the fittings. You need to be able to spit out your toothpaste or wash your face in the basin without bashing your head on the bathroom cabinet. No matter how tight for space your bathroom is, it needs to be comfortable and easy to use.

The first rule is do not over fill your bathroom; more is not always better. If you cannot comfortably fit a shower cubicle in to your family bathroom then you are better off with a shower over the bath. Large spa baths and bidets may read like luxury items on your property's description but if they are shoehorned into a space that is clearly not big enough they will not be popular with buyers.

All shower taps should be easily accessible from outside the shower area, *(so you don't have to stand under the shower to adjust the temperature, which can lead to burns)*. Your bathroom should be well ventilated with an adequate extractor fan, and have enough heating. Towel rails and hooks should be easy to reach from the shower or bath.

Lighting and mirrors should be adequate for shaving and makeup and there should be enough storage and surface space for conducting general ablutions, *(for this reason I tend to prefer a vanity unit to a pedestal basin).*

Bathrooms are expensive to redecorate, so if you are renovating for sale try to choose something that will have the broadest possible appeal. I tend to avoid big bold colour statements or overly distinctive feature tiles as they may put some buyers off. It is better to go for more neutral tiles and fittings and dress the room with coloured towels, soap dishes, artworks and planters.

Too Masculine

Women make most purchasing decisions so unless you are pitching your property specifically to the bachelor or gay market I would avoid making the bathrooms too dark or masculine. You don't want women to feel alienated by your choices, *(although you don't want to be too overtly feminine either)*. If you are aiming for the broadest possible market try to keep it gender neutral and family friendly.

Family Friendly

Toilets:

Wall faced toilet suites, where the all pipes and bends are concealed within a smooth porcelain casing, are a must these days in any mid to top end renovation. They used to be very expensive but in recent years the price has come right down so there is no excuse for not using one. These days I use wall-faced suites even in budget properties. They give a high-end designer look and are much easier to keep clean.

Most wall-faced units are designed to work as an "S" trap *(connects through the floor)* or a "P" trap *(connects through the wall)*, and come complete with the necessary adaptor. They usually accommodate a wide range of **"set backs"**, *(a set back is the distance from the wall to the centre of the waste pipe in the floor, also known as the "rough in" distance)*. If however you are choosing a non wall-faced unit, make sure you buy the correct "S" or "P" trap configuration to meet your requirements.

Close-coupled toilet suites:

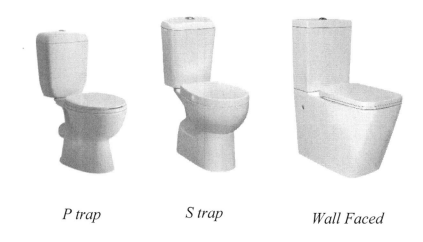

P trap   *S trap*   *Wall Faced*

All "S" trap toilets have a prescribed set-back *(or rough-in distance)*. This is a critical measurement if you are using a

"close coupled"* suite as the cistern must sit on the back of the pan and against the wall. You need to take care to check the set-back on a close coupled suite before you buy it as there is usually no more than an inch latitude in this measurement. The metric standard is 150mm, and the US imperial standard is 12.5inches, however different suites have different set backs so don't just assume any toilet will fit. *(a close coupled suite is a ceramic suite where the cistern is designed to sit on the back of the pan and the two units are "coupled" together).

However if you are installing an ultra budget "S" trap suite, (usually with a plastic cistern), it will most probably use a flush pipe that can be adjusted to accommodate a wide range of set-backs.

Toilets with flush pipes

While such options will usually look cheaper, if you are faced with an unusual set back and don't want to go to the expense of resetting the plumbing a flush pipe unit can get you out of a difficult and expensive problem, *(there are however some more expensive period options with metal flush pipes that can be quite attractive in the right setting).*

A more designer high-end alternative would be to box out over the floor drain and use a wall-hung toilet. With this type of toilet the cistern is concealed in the wall. In some places it is quite common for wall-hung toilets to be integrated into a larger vanity and basin unit.

Wall Hung with Vanity   *Wall Hung*

Flexible or offset pan connectors are another option your plumber can use to get around the problem of an awkward set back.

Whether or not it is a requirement in your area, always go for a dual flush unit. With increasing populations, and persistent water shortages it is highly likely dual flush units will become mandatory everywhere over the next few years. Quite aside from the fact that environmental concerns are high on people's minds these days, having a single flush toilet may date your bathroom and need to be replaced down the track. There can be no doubt that the cost of a domestic water supply is only going to increase, and as installing a dual flush unit will not put any buyers off and costs no more than a single flush, there really is no excuse for not using one.

Shower Screens:

Frameless shower screens are a must have in a top-end renovation but they are considerably more expensive than the fully framed or semi frameless alternatives. Fully framed shower screens tend to be seen as being a bit down market these days, so I would generally avoid using one, *(although I might consider it in a budget rental)*.

For a mid range property you are unlikely to get a return on the high cost of going frameless, but a semi frameless screen is usually just fine. I would use a semi frameless screen even in a low-end property if the budget permitted.

If you are using a wet room shower base, and you have the space to configure it as a walk in shower, you may be able to get away with a single frameless fixed panel. This can give you that high-end designer frameless look at a significantly cheaper price.

Note: If you are installing a new bathroom, (and your walls are not brick), do not forget to install a timber stud in the wall so there is something to screw into to support your shower screen.

Baths:

Whether you go for free standing, wall set, or hob mounted; steel, cast iron or acrylic, every family home should have at least one bath.

If you have a wonderful deep old cast iron bath you may choose to keep it and get it professionally resurfaced, which often looks great and can save you hundreds of dollars. The process is fairly straightforward and usually takes a couple of days from start to finish. This is a job for a professional bath re-surfacer, I do not recommend attempting this yourself, nor do I recommend painting a bath. It never looks good and it never lasts.

Free Standing Bath

Freestanding baths are not suitable for small bathrooms. They tend to cost a lot more than hob set or wall set baths and are mostly used in high-end properties. If you are renovating your own home you may want to consider the extra work involved in cleaning around and under a freestanding bath, particularly claw-foot baths, before you install one.

Hob mounted baths are not suitable where there is a shower over the bath, as water will pool in the corners of the hob and lead to dirt, mould, leaks and rot in your bath frame. If you are having a shower over your bath you need to set it hard up against the wall.

Hob Set Bath

Shower Over Bath

Basins and Vanities:

My personal preference is for a vanity unit. While pedestal basins can be good for achieving a period look they often leave pipe work visible and do not provide any storage or surface space. By contrast vanity units offer a lot of storage and surface space, conceal the plumbing, and many offer the option of his and hers basins *(space permitting)*. There are a wide range of colours and styles available and you can generally find one that will fit with your decor.

If you are going to install a vanity I recommend using either a wall hung unit or one mounted on legs. A floor standing vanity can be subject to water damage, rot and swelling. Once a vanity unit has swelled it cannot be repaired and will need to be replaced. However if you already have a vanity that sits on the floor, make sure you use a mildew resistant silicone to caulk around the base of the unit as this will help to prevent moisture from getting in and causing problems.

Wall Hung Vanity   *Floor Standing*

While many people chose to have a flat mirror hung over the basin, it is not uncommon to have a shaving cabinet or shelf mounted directly over the basin. If a cabinet or shelf is too low, or protrudes too far out this can make accessing the sink awkward and uncomfortable. If you are using a shaving cabinet I recommend you recess it into the wall if possible.

Vanity on Legs

Floor wastes and overflows:

Some baths and sinks come with an inbuilt "overflow", which will automatically drain any water that rises above a certain level. While such overflows are excellent for preventing floods it is also worth putting in a floor waste as a precautionary measure to drain any accidental overflows.

Floor Waste

Even if you have an overflow in your sink and bath there is still a chance a washing machine or toilet may overflow and cause problems.

If you are renovating a bathroom or laundry installing a floor waste is not a big expense and well worth it for the protection it provides. This is particularly important in an upstairs bathroom as there may be lighting or electrical wires between the floor and downstairs ceiling, and any flooding could cause electrocution if you do not have adequate circuit-breakers.

TILES AND TILING

While there are many different types of tiles, such as glass, porcelain or marble, the most common type of tiles are ceramic. Ceramic tiles are either made of kiln fired clay or porcelain with a coloured glaze set on the surface. They may be cushion or round edged, *(where there is a slight rebate on the edge of the tile),* or rectified *(where the tile surface is flat from edge to edge).*

Cushion edged tiles, particularly those with wavy edges, are a far more forgiving choice for DIYer's as they do not require the same level of precision to lay as rectified tiles.

Ceramic tiles can be sealed so the surface is impervious to moisture, or unsealed. When selecting tiles make sure to find out if the tile you intend to use is sealed. If you are using unsealed tiles, such as unpolished travertine, slate or raw terracotta, *(something I do not recommend),* you will need to seal them immediately after laying as they will take on dirt and stains very quickly.

There are low VOC* water based sealers available but they do not generally wear all that well, *(you will have to reseal your tiles every 2-3 years, depending on traffic).* High VOC polyurethane based sealers have a longer life but they require a turpentine based clean up, longer drying times and are more difficult to work with. If it is at all possible get honed or sealed tiles, as they will give you years of trouble free performance.

* VOC stands for volatile organic compounds.

I recommend getting a professional tiler, as a less than optimal tiling job can make your entire renovation appear cheap and shoddy. If however you are determined to DIY it there are some tips to bear in mind.

1. Make sure you get your substrate solid, level and straight. This is particularly crucial if you are using larger tiles.

2. Make sure you properly water proof all wet areas. The methods of waterproofing vary widely from place to place; it can be as full-on as laying fibre glass webbing fabric and sealing it with a waterproof rubberised mastic paint, or as little as simply applying a couple of coats of PVA glue, so you will need to consult with your local tile or hardware professionals to find out how it is done in your area.

As the UK tends to be light on waterproofing I would strongly recommend you install a wet room shower base, or a pre fabricated shower base unit for tiling over. Water leaks in shower bases have been known to rot the floor out and cause catastrophic collapses.

3. Ideally you would fix any floor movement before you start tiling, but unless you are working on a concrete floor there will always be some amount of spring. Laying ply or cement sheeting over floorboards as a substrate is not enough to totally prevent any movement from occurring in the floor. Using a *"flexible tile adhesive"* will allow for that small amount of movement and help prevent any cracking in the tiles. I would avoid using very large tiles over anything other than concrete as they will be far more prone to cracking.

4. Plan it out before you start. There is nothing worse than having a tile wall finish with a slice of tile that is only 1/2 an inch wide. Divide the length of the wall by the tile size plus grout gap, and work out how many tiles it will take. If your measure is say 15.1, tiles across you definitely won't want to start with a whole tile, as the .1 tile you are left with at the other end will be hard to cut and will look awful. You would be better to start and finish with a tile .55 wide.

Also be aware of any taps or power points you may have to allow for. Ideally your tap holes will fall either on the very edge of the tile, or in the centre of the tile. You don't want to be trying to cut a hole right near the edge of a tile.

Cutting holes in tiles can be tricky. It may be worth checking with your local tile suppliers as some now offer a cutting service for tap holes. There are also diamond tipped drill bits and cutting disks for your angle grinder that can make the process easier.

5. Check your starting levels. Do not assume that all surfaces on the same plane are in fact parallel. Check the floor, the ceiling and the bath as they may not all be level and parallel. *(Usually this problem will only occur if you are reusing the existing fittings, as if you are installing new you would get them totally level).* If you find that things are not level then you need to assess which plane you are going to level your tiles to.

If you are tiling around a shower bath, and the bath is not quite parallel to the ceiling it will probably better to take the ceiling line as level, as the variation in levels will be less obvious. To have your tiles finish parallel with the ceiling you would need to make slight length adjustments to your first line of tiles over the bath.

If you suspect you have, or will have this problem, I recommend you match your tile colour as closely as you can to the colour of your fixtures, *(which will usually leave you with white on white).* This will make any slight anomaly very hard to detect. *(If you want to punch up the colour, you can use your floor tiles, towels, bath mats and other decor dressings).*

6. Use tile spacers, but don't be a slave to them. Often there will be slight anomalies in the substrate, particularly in old houses,

that you simply cannot fix. If that is the case then you will need to tweak the spaces to accommodate for the anomalies. I have seen may tilers shave a little off the edge of a spacer, or replace a spacer with matches that they can split to create the desired gap.

If you have a substrate that is impossible to make straight and level, it is better to go for smaller tiles with non-uniform edges. However if you really want straight edged tiles then matching the grout colour to the tiles can go a long way to disappearing any problems.

7. Use mould resistant grout and silicone. Seal your grout before you use the area and make sure you silicone any corner joins, bath and shower base edges to get a waterproof seal. *(Whatever you do, don't grout corners, bath or shower base edges!)* You should always fill the bath before you silicone it, as many baths will drop down a couple of millimetres when full. Filling the bath before you silicone will ensure that your seal will remain watertight once the bath is regular use.

PLASTER

Patchy walls and crumbling plaster will need to be dealt with. If you have a lot of loose and flaky plaster you may want to pull it off before re-plastering. If the existing plaster is solid, or there are lathes you can screw new plasterboard to, you may wish to skim coat or dry wall straight over the top. Be aware that if you do plaster or dry wall over the top, your door jams may need to be packed out or replaced, as you will be adding to the width of the wall.

Do not be afraid of loosing decorative plasterwork in period properties. Most period mouldings, corbels and ceiling roses can be replaced with new replicas, which will give a top end finish. Many of these are surprisingly inexpensive and give a genuine period look.

Outdated, textured ceilings may be okay in a rental property but they are not popular with buyers. There are a few options for dealing with the textured ceilings, from skimming over them or scraping them back to covering them with fresh drywall. If you choose to scrape them back be aware of the date of the property as some of the older texture coats, like vermiculite, can contain asbestos. If you are in any doubt take a sample for testing. If you have asbestos it may be best to simply skim coat or dry wall over it.

In deciding on what crown mouldings *(or cornices)* and roses to use take the style and age of the property into account and make sure your choice is appropriate to your ceiling height. An oversized crown moulding on a low ceiling will give an oppressive effect, as will an oversized ceiling rose in a tiny room. These days many modern renovations are foregoing crown mouldings all together in favour of a square set finish, *(square set is the same right angle finish you would find in the corner of a room).*

Unless you are a skilled plasterer or dry-waller don't DIY it. It will take you forever and a poor finish will compromise your sale price. Professional plastering is usually a very good investment, as it is not at all expensive compared to the increased value fresh smooth walls will add to your house.

Floors and floor coverings

Your choice of flooring is often dictated by the weather conditions in your area. While ceramic tiles are understandably popular in the tropics they can be very unwelcoming in the colder climes. But weather is not the only consideration. Cleaning, durability, underfoot feel, and acoustics can be just as important. If you have very high ceilings or a lot of glass, a hard tile floor can make a room very loud and acoustically bright. Is this a problem? Would you be better with timber, or maybe cork or vinyl if you want it even quieter?

When choosing floor colours, mid tones are best. If you go too light or too dark with your floors every crumb and speck of dust will scream at you. High gloss timber finishes are great for increasing light levels but show more of the dust.

Carpet:

While carpet is not as popular as it once was, there are places where it is still loved and appreciated. While I do not recommend fitted carpet for high traffic living areas, fresh carpet has an opulent plush foot feel which can be quite lovely in a bedroom.

If your house is in an area where the market expects to have fitted carpet in the living areas, do not put carpet just inside an external doorway. No matter how well people wipe their feet, wet dirty shoes will ruin your entry way very quickly. It can even start to get shabby during your buyer inspections. If you do not have a vestibule or portico where guests can remove their shoes then a small entry landing of tiles or timber just inside the door is absolutely essential.

Buy the best quality underlay you can afford. A good looking but inexpensive carpet with a quality thick underlay will give a far better impression than an expensive carpet laid on cheap thin underlay. It's all about the under foot feel.

Whether you are going for a loop pile, shag pile or cut pile, there are some great looking man-made fibres that are wonderfully hardwearing and quite inexpensive; although for a quality look and feel you cannot beat wool. I tend to prefer an 80/20 wool blend to pure wool as it is more stain resistant and is considerably more durable. If renovating for sale I would avoid a carpet with dominant colours or patterns.

Timber:

Sprung floorboards: Sprung floorboards are tongue and groove boards that are laid over floor joists or particleboard flooring. They tend to have a small amount of movement in them, which gives a slight spring to them, thus the term "sprung" floor.

You can also glue floor boards directly to concrete but it is not something that is broadly recommended; if you have the ceiling height to loose a couple of inches it is far better to bolt timber battens onto the concrete and lay your boards as a sprung floor.

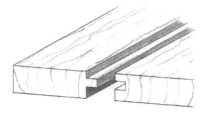

Tongue and groove floorboards

Regardless of whether you secret nail *(where you nail through the tongue and the surface of the board is left clear)*, or top nail *(where the nails are driven through the top face of the board)*, you should also glue all boards down with a strong construction adhesive to avoid squeaks in the finished floor, *(if your carpenter is laying your floor INSIST that he glues your boards as well as nailing them)*.

If you are using wide boards it is advisable to top nail as wider boards that have been secret nailed have a tendency to cup.

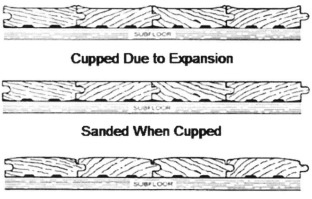

Cupped Due to Expansion

Sanded When Cupped

Crowned Once the Floor Dries

When you are buying your floor boards make sure that the boards have been stored correctly *(not out in the weather)*, and that they have been properly kiln dried to the correct moisture content, as boards that are too wet may crown when they dry out and boards that are too dry may cup after they are laid. It is standard practice to season floorboards by storing them in the house for at least 2 weeks before you lay them, so they can acclimatise to the ambient temperature and humidity of the property. I highly recommend this, *(this is particularly important for glued down floor boards).*

Floorboards come in a range of *"qualities"*, and this can determine the price. Boards with more knots, streaks and visible grains tend to be cheaper than clear unblemished timer. There are however some floor boards, such as soft plantation pine boards, that are not suitable for polishing as they are not hard enough to take the wear and tear of daily foot traffic; even some of the hardwood boards are more of a utility grade, and are really only suitable for replacing broken boards that you intend to cover over.

If you are laying raw floorboards for a timber floor you will have to sand and seal them. If you are sanding and polishing your floors know that it will take up to a week and in that time you will not be able to access the property or carry on any other internal work.

There are high gloss and satin finishing products available in both high *(oil based)* and low *(water based)* VOC formulations. Oil based finishes are far harder wearing and there are some additive hardeners or two pack varieties you can use for maximum durability. Water based finishes have greatly improved in quality over the past decade to the point where they are a good option, hardwearing in a domestic setting. Water based products will dry a lot faster and are much less toxic to use.

There are also many colour tints, stains and lime washing products you can add to your finish to get a unique look. Darker coloured floors tend to be less forgiving of dust and general living and will require more regular maintenance to look their best.

If you are working on an older house and you have pulled up your carpets to discover you have black painted floors around the edges, you most likely have "Black Japan" (an old tar based paint) on your floors. While this can be sanded off, be aware a professional sander will charge you considerably more for doing so. If you decide to DIY it it will be a long and difficult job and you will need a lot of extra sand paper.

Parquetry: Parquetry is the ultimate in luxury timber flooring. It is by far the most expensive of all timber floors and not something I would not attempt to DIY. While there are some standard patterns that are relatively affordable the range of designs and inlays are as limitless as your imagination.

Bamboo Floorboards: Bamboo floorboards generally come pre finished in a wonderful range of tones and colours. As it grows so fast bamboo is a very eco friendly choice. It is extremely hard and durable, quick to lay, and is great way to give a timber finish to a concrete floor. Like all floating floors you will need to lay it over the correct underlay on clear flat surface.

If you are laying a floating floor over a ground floor concrete slab and you are uncertain of the moisture levels in the concrete, you should use an underlay that has a moisture barrier built in.

Engineered floating floors: Engineered floating floors are constructed from a pre finished solid timber veneer mounted on a ply wood substrate. While not quite as environmentally friendly as bamboo, they can be very beautiful and hardwearing. They are a less expensive way to finish a floor with an expensive timber and offer a wider range of looks and finishes than standard floorboards.

Vinyl flooring:

Vinyl flooring has not been all that popular in recent years, although it has had somewhat of a resurgence with the introduction of DIY vinyl floor planks. Vinyl floorboards are a good cheap way to give a timber floor look to a budget or rental property.

Recently some designers have begun to use vinyl in their renovations due to the huge range of patters and colours available. There are even companies, such as Murafloor in the UK and Graphic Image Flooring in the USA that will print your own custom designs.

Vinyl can be a good choice for utility areas, bathrooms and kitchens, particularly if you live in a cold climate and heating is an issue. Vinyl is much warmer underfoot than tiles and it is also a relatively quiet floor. Vinyl is available in a range of widths, so for most rooms you should be able to install it without a join.

There is a huge variation in the quality of vinyls and I would not recommend installing a cheaper product anywhere that you expect a reasonable amount of foot traffic, as cheaper vinyls tend to tear easily.

It is important to have a clean clear flat surface when installing, otherwise you will end up with lumps and tears. If you are installing over ceramic tiles or floorboards you should always lay down a plywood, cement sheet or Masonite substrate first.

LIGHT FITTINGS

Unlike carpet, tiles and counter tops, *(that are difficult and expensive to replace)*, light fittings are one area where I think it is ok to express a more risky personal aesthetic. While light fittings can be very expensive, you can get a good range of choices without spending a lot; so if a buyer doesn't like your choice it's a relatively simple matter for them to change it.

In many places the price of electricity is skyrocketing, so no matter what type of lighting you are putting in you should be mindful of how much power it uses. Is there a more energy efficient alternative that looks just as good? Even in the higher income brackets people are far more concerned with their carbon footprint and energy consumption these days.

Drop Ceiling lights: Drop ceiling lights, also known as pendant lights, hang down from the ceiling. If you are planning to install new pendant lights, or change the position of existing ones, make sure the electrician checks that there is a timber in the ceiling to hang the light from. You cannot generally hang the weight of a pendant light fitting off unsupported dry wall.

Flush mount lights: Flush mount lights, also known as oyster lights, are lights that sit flat to the ceiling. Some flush mount lights have very little weight in them so you may be able to fit one to dry wall with the proper screws and plugs. They are great for low ceilings.

Wall sconces: A wall sconce is as the name suggests a wall mounted light. These can give a great effect but you will have to get the wiring done, and make sure you have noggins in place to take the weight of the fitting before any plaster work is finished off.

Down-lights: While some buyers consider down-lights a must have designer item, others do not like them at all, so if you are intent on using down-lights you might consider installing some pendant lights or wall sconces as well, so buyers who are not fond of down-lights won't be put off.

Banks of halogen down-lights cost a lot of money to run and that can be a real turn off for some buyers. If you are putting in new down lights, try to use the new LED low energy type, *(and let your buyers know they are energy efficient)*.

The energy efficient down-lights are more expensive to buy up front, but well worth the investment. If your property already has down-lights that use GU10 Globes you can easily switch them out for the new LED globes, but if your down-lights are low voltage and use the MR16 globes you may need to change the transformers if you want switch them over, *(many of the old electronic transformers will not work with the new LED globes).*

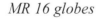

MR 16 globes   *GU10 globes*

Another reason to opt for the new LED down-lights is that they do not run as hot. Halogen down-lights can reach scorching temperatures and are responsible for hundreds of house fires every year. If you are installing halogens make sure any wiring or insulation you use is set well back away from the globes and are suitably fire proof.

Fluorescent lights: While the newer warm white compact fluorescent globes may find a place in various light fittings throughout the home, keep traditional fluorescent light fittings limited to use in the garage. Enough said!

COLOURS AND DECOR

Colour choice is deeply personal and what resonates for one person may put someone else off. When renovating for sale or even with a view to selling down the track it pays to be mindful of the market when making your choices.

Some people are acutely sensitive to colour and a shade that is even a little off the mark can give a negative impression of a house without a buyer even knowing why they didn't like it. As a rule I keep the walls neutral, no more than one to two tones off white, matched with neutral mid tone or timber floors. A wall shade that is just off white is likely to appeal to the widest range of buyers and not put anyone off.

That said, white is not just white. There are literally thousands of shades of off white, and each one has it's own personality. For a renovation for sale I prefer the stone, beige, green and grey toned whites rather than the red, yellow or blue toned ones. The reason for this is that red, yellow and blue, being primary colours, are quite dominant tones, and will dictate what colours one can match with your decor.

For example if you paint in a very pale blue and the buyer has an expensive terracotta couch, they may be put off because they feel their furniture will clash with the decor and they don't want to have to repaint. However if you had used in a less dominant tone no matter what colour their furniture and art works are they are unlikely to clash with your chosen wall colours.

Another advantage of the neutral tones is that you can dress different rooms with different colours. For example I have painted houses with one wall colour, but dressed the master bedroom with gold and brown toned soft furnishings and artworks, pink for the girl's room, blue for the boy's room, and fresh green tones for the living areas. This way you can show your buyer that no matter what their furnishings and colour preferences your home will accommodate their taste without them having to repaint.

If you are one of those people for whom white is just white and you really can't see much difference between shades it may be worth investing in a colour consultant. A good colour consultant will know what shades will work in your space.

Generally speaking I avoid premixed colours. While there are some stunning premix colours available, *(I love Dulux UK's "Egyptian cotton" for example)*, they are far and few between. You will often find much more expensive looking designer colours in the tint to order ranges. Many paint stores now offer a computer matching service that allows you to have paint tinted to match any colour sample, so you can match your paint to the colour in your sofa or a cushion if you want to.

What ever colour you chose for your walls get a sample pot, and paint a reasonable sized sample on several different walls before you purchase in bulk. The lighting conditions in many retail outlets can alter your perception of a colour and it may look very different on your wall. Also different walls in your house have different levels of light and shade, and what looks great in one room may not suit another room.

Try to keep a consistent tone throughout the property. If you really want a little more colour in the bedroom you could consider a double strength tint, but once again get a tester pot first.

Wallpaper: As a rule I avoid wallpaper. It is expensive, difficult to hang well and no matter what you chose at least 35% of your potential buyers won't like it.

However if you love wallpaper and really want to make a bold statement with the colour, I suggest you buy a large artists canvas from a variety store and wallpaper that instead. It will give you all the colour and pattern you are after, but any buyer that doesn't like it will not be put off by something that is as easily removed as a painting.

You can also get removable wallpaper and decals, but if you are going to use them make sure your agent tells potential buyers that they are in fact removable.

PAINTING

Painting is one of the best things you can do to give your property an instant lift and freshen, It is also a task that many people feel confident to DIY. But it is not something you should rush into unprepared as there are many considerations to take into account and many tips and tricks to getting a top notch finish.

Most of your painting time should go on surface preparation. Washing down all surfaced with sugar soap, scraping back any loose and flaking paint and filling and sanding all the cracks and dents is absolutely essential if you want a professional result. If there are any water stains, or there has been mould or mildew on your walls you should prime the surface with a stain blocking or mould resistant undercoat sealer to stop the problem reoccurring. *(I recommend Zinnser products as they are broadly available and very effective).* If you are painting over old paint there are many primers such as ESP or Penetrol that can help the paint key into the old surface and prevent peeling and blistering.

Before you select your paint you should access the quality of your surface. Patchy or rough walls will always look better with a flat, eggshell or low sheen finish, as a high gloss finish will highlight any surface imperfections. While it is traditional to paint woodwork and doors in high gloss, if your woodwork is old, uneven and dented it may also look better with a lower sheen finish.

Better quality paints will usually wear far better, but as a general rule the lower the sheen level the less washable the finish. You should be able to wash marks of a satin finish, whereas a flat paint will usually mark when wiped down. As ceilings don't usually get scuffed they should be painted with as flat a finish as possible to help hide any imperfections in your plasterwork, *(in most areas there are specially formulated "ceiling paints" available)*. Conversely kitchen walls are subject to stains and cooking grease, and as such a satin finish will be far more durable.

Do you need an undercoat or sealer? Raw timber, fresh plaster or dry wall will require some kind of primer sealer. While skim coat or hard plaster can often be sealed with normal wall paint, dry wall will require a specially formulated undercoat sealer. Many modern paint formulations have a built in primer sealer, but not all so check before you buy.

New wood should be sanded before painting, but even so the first coat will always *"raise the grain"*. This is where the wood drinks in the paint and swells slightly leaving the surface rough to the touch. This is not a cause for panic as once you have sanded it back again subsequent coats should leave a smooth finish.

There are two main types of paint formulations available.

High VOC: These are your oil-based polyurethanes and estapols. Long wearing and durable, especially in external applications, they require a long drying time, turpentine clean up and a well ventilated work area. They are particularly good for ultra glossy finishes but are prone to yellowing over time.

Low VOC: These are water-based emulsions, eggshells, plastic, vinyl and acrylic paints. They have a quick drying time, water clean up and are generally safer to use in enclosed spaces. They have long been used for walls, but some of the more recent formulations work wonderfully on woodwork as well.

When making your choice it is a matter of taking all the factors into account and working out what will best suit your project.

Painting walls: When painting walls you will either use a spray gun or a roller. As spray guns are best left to the professionals I am going to confine my advice to painting with a roller.

Get the best quality equipment that you can afford. Cheap roller frames are no end of trouble. They often don't roll smoothly, leaving a patchy application and if you apply a decent amount of pressure to them they tend to fall apart. They also have a tendency to collect paint in the roller end, which seeps out to leave raised or feathered streaks along the edges of the roller line.

The roller tray should have a reasonable amount of weight in it and be able to hold a decent amount of paint in its storage well. It should have pronounced groves on the draining tray. Some of the cheaper, lightweight units have an almost flat tray, which makes it difficult to spread the paint evenly on the roller. If there is not enough weight in the tray it will often lift slightly when you try to spread the paint evenly on the roller. This makes loading the roller properly quite difficult and often causes spills.

When using cheap paint trays many people end up applying more pressure on the roller and tray in an attempt to get an even spread of paint on their roller, which can result in the tray cracking or breaking. Trust me you do not want a broken paint tray leaking its contents out onto your floor. A decent paint tray and roller only cost a few dollars more but what they will save you in time and aggravation is immeasurable.

While it is ok not to spend a fortune on roller covers, be aware that many of the cheaper ones will shed fluff and leave little hairy blotches on your freshly painted surface. If using a cheaper roller cover you can reduce this problem significantly by combing it with a fine pet brush to remove all the loose fluff before you begin. You should however keep an eye on your wall to make sure that any stray bits of fluff are spotted, removed and re-rolled before your paint dries.

You will need to choose the correct roller for your surface. Choose a long nap (long hair) roller for rough, textured surfaces such as brick work or stippled ceilings, a short to medium nap for flat walls and a dense foam roller for any high gloss surfaces.

When painting walls always use a roller pole. If you are doing any more than one room I recommend you invest in a solid, adjustable aluminium painting pole, rather than using one of the cheap wooden ones. It will last much longer, and being adjustable it will make the job much easier. When painting with a pole you should always wear a pair of tight fitting rubber faced gardening gloves to give extra traction and prevent blisters.

Load your roller by dipping it into the paint well and then rolling it back and forwards over the grooved part of the tray until the roller is evenly loaded with paint. Do not overload your roller. If you do there will not be enough traction on the wall for the roller to spin, or you will end up with a lot of spatter.

Starting in one corner of the room place your roller as close to the ceiling as you can without touching it, then roll straight down to the bottom of the wall. If you have loaded your roller right and applied the correct amount of pressure there should now be a solid block of paint where you have run the roller. If not return to the top and repeat until the strip is properly covered.

Once the first strip is adequately covered move over about 2/3's of the roller width and repeat, so you are repainting the last 1/3 of the previous strip, and painting 2/3's of a new strip. Continue this process until the roller is no longer covering the new strip, and then reload with paint. On average you should be able to do 2-3 strips on a single load, depending of course on your ceiling height and how porous and thirsty the walls are.

After you have done 2-3 strips stand back and examine the wall. Often there will be visible feathering lines in the paint where the roller's edge was. If so, go back to the start of the section and roll over it again using the same method, only this time apply some pressure to the outside edge of the roller, *(If you are painting out towards the right from the corner put pressure on the right side of the roller, if you are moving towards the left, then you put pressure on the left side).*

This will leave a distinct feathering on the side you are applying pressure to, but it will remove any trace of feathering on the other side, leaving you with a flat even paint surface. You should gently ease off the pressure on your roller as you get to the top or bottom of the wall to avoid leaving feathering lines around your ceiling and floor cutting in lines.

When you get to a window or door or the end of the wall you can get rid of the last line of feathering by cutting in the edge or running your paintbrush into the corner, *(something you would have to do anyway)*. If you follow this method you should end up with a good even coverage, without any visible streaking, roller marks or shadows.

When working with a roller you should always run your paintbrush down the corners before the paint from your roller dries to remove any lumps of drips.

Once you have rolled your walls you will need to cut in your top and bottom edges. If you are painting an entire house it will be worth investing in some work platforms, *(I recommend a minimum of 3 but 4 or five is better).* You can pick work platforms up at Home Depot or any bulk hardware store without spending an arm or a leg.

Trust me, work platforms will save you hours of time and make the job much less physically taxing. Inching a ladder around the room to cut in a ceiling 3 foot at a time is a mugs game, particularly when you take into account that you will have to do it on average 3-4 times for each room. When using work platforms you simply set them up around the room and just walk around to do your cutting in. A job that can easily take 2 hours with a ladder can take as little as 10 minutes with work platforms.

Before cutting in you need to make sure the wall coat is dry, as going over half dry paint will pull it from the wall and create bumps in the surface. You will need a small pot of paint with a handle, *(one that you can easily carry, do not try to take the big tin around with you)*, and a good quality cutting in brush.

Do not use cheap brushes. It is a false economy. They shed bristles, and worse the bristles bend and skew making it impossible to get a good line. A good paint brush is an investment in a quality finish and if you look after it it will last for many years.

For cutting in I recommend using an angled sash brush, about 2 – 3 inches wide.

Angled Sash Brush

Load up your brush, taking care to wipe any excess paint off *(you don't want any runs or drips).* Place the brush just below the ceiling line and easy it up at an angle into the corner, then pull the brush towards the narrow end. It will take a few goes to get the feel of it but with a bit of practice you should be able to cut in like a pro. If you make a few slips at the start you can always go back over them. I find the tiny brushes you get in the brush sets they sell at dime stores can be excellent for covering over small slips.

I like to keep a roll of plastic cling wrap handy to wrap rollers or paint brushes in between coats. If you squeeze out all the air the cling wrap will stop the paint setting in your brush or roller. This can save you a lot of time cleaning brushes and rollers, as they will only need to be thoroughly washed at the end of the day.

Decent drop cloths are essential. The light-weight plastic sheets that you buy for $1 are only really suitable as dust covers for furnishings. They do not have sufficient weight to stay put on a floor and will kick up and fold over at the slightest movement, spreading any paint drips directly onto your floor. They also tear easily and are generally not strong enough to endure the moving of a ladder. Old sheets are often not thick enough to absorb any drips and you will find small spots where the paint has seeped through. If you must use old sheets try to fold them so you have at least a double thickness.

The best solution is thick professional drops cloths. They are expensive but will protect your floors. However if you are determined to improvise the best option is old black out curtains. The black out backing makes them thick and largely impervious to seeping paint. You can usually get a set for next to nothing from the local charity store.

Lead paint: Lead was one of the main ingredients in paint up until the 70's. Lead is now recognised to be highly toxic and as such one should always exercise due caution when attempting to remediate old painted surfaces. Do not sand surfaces painted with lead paint (if in doubt take a sample to be tested by your local environmental testing agent). You are better to remove lead paint with a heat gun and scrape it back. If you are scraping back led paint make sure to wear a good ventilating mask. Gather up all the scrapings and dispose of them properly, do not allow lead paint flakes to mix in with the soil. In some parts of the USA there are strict regulations regarding the remediation of lead paint, and any remediation may need to be certified so check with your local authority as to what is required.

WINDOW TREATMENTS

Window dressings can cost a little or a lot, but the choices you make shouldn't be determined just by budget. There are a few guiding principles that you should follow when making your selection.

Whether you choose curtains or blinds, all bedrooms windows and any window that faces the street should have two levels of window treatment, one sheer and one block out. This will give the maximum flexibility in terms of privacy, light control, and view. Bathroom windows that are not made of obscured glass should always have a full block out option. While in some circumstances it is conventional to provide them, windows facing a private back garden do not necessarily need any window treatments at all.

Each type of window treatment has it's own advantages and disadvantages.

Blinds:

Venetian blinds: On the positive they can provide total block out privacy or a view through the whole window. On the negative they are dust catchers and difficult to keep clean. They can be difficult to open fully, and the slats can get bent.

Holland blinds: On the positive they are stylish and up market looking. On the negative, they cannot be opened fully to reveal the whole window and do not provide any privacy when open.

Vertical blinds: On the positive they can provide block out or shielded privacy and are easy to draw back to uncover the whole window. On the negative they are a bit dated and tend to get tangled up.

Roller blinds: On the positive they are easy to operate, can open fully, come in both sheer and block out options, or you can have both in one blind.

Plantation Shutters: On the positive they are appealing to buyers, provide some level of sound and temperature insulation, provide both full block out and partial view. On the negative they can be bulky and difficult to clean, and can reduce the overall light level available.

Curtains:

Tab top: On the positive, inexpensive, quick and easy, on the negative they don't always hang well and can be difficult to open to and close.

Pinch and pencil pleat: Pinch and pencil pleat curtains run on a track, and require hooks and rings. They are more complex to install but are easy to draw. Pencil pleats look better if you are not using a pelmet as they have a neater top edge.

Eyelet: Large eyelets have become popular over recent years as they are very quick and easy to fit and draw well. Like tab tops they usually come ready made. When using eyelet curtains make sure to use a curtain rod with a large diameter, as eyelets on a narrow rod look totally wrong.

Rod pocket: Rod pocket curtains are not optimum if you want to open and close them regularly as they are tricky to open and close as they are prone to bunching up on the rod. They are however good for bedroom privacy sheers that sit in front of a block out blind.

When renovating for sale I don't like to spend too heavily on window treatments. Like wallpaper, curtains that make a strong statement will put some buyers off. I prefer to use neutrally coloured full block out roller blinds along with plain white sheers. This is an inexpensive window treatment that looks very appealing and goes with any decor.

When looking at roller blinds I prefer the ones with the metal pull cords as I think they look far more upmarket than the plastic ones. Ikea's VIVAN range of white sheers comes at a very modest price and can be used as a rod pocket, concealed tab top, or pinch pleat curtain. I use them often and to great effect.

GARDENS AND LANDSCAPES

A good garden can literally add thousands of dollars to your sale price so if you are doing a renovation for sale start working on the garden as soon as you possibly can.

Plants need time to establish and will often look quite wilted while after they are first planted out. If you wait until just before you are on the market to do your planting you may end up presenting buyers with a sea of sad and stressed out plants. You need to give any trees and shrubs you are putting in time to root down, and for any turf you have laid to be past the stage where it might be turning brown at the edges.

Gardens can be expensive so if your budget is limited, or your property is in an area where privacy fencing is not used, I would concentrate my efforts on the front garden and street appeal. For inner city brown stone or terrace style houses colourful window boxes and hanging baskets give great street appeal.

For more suburban homes, good fencing (if applicable to your area), good lawns, and a well-defined path are essential. If you are putting in a new path try not to have it run in a straight line from the gate to the door. Although no one really knows why a curved or offset path with a bend is always more appealing, and just tends to feel better to buyers.

Try to get some height variation into your garden, either with built up garden beds, trees or shrubs as this gives a very pleasing effect. Vertical gardens can be used to great effect if space is tight. You can also give a small area a very expansive feel with a well-placed mirror.

Decking: People love decking, and a good sized deck will always earn it's money back, but if you have a small or less expensive property you do not have to do anything large or elaborate to give the sense of a "decked area". Even a small decked landing area can add a great deal of charm.

If you do not have the room or the budget for a large raised deck there are a number of cheap easy options for adding that decking ambience to your garden. If you have a concrete patio you can do a very cheap easy deck over with clip-together decking tiles, or if you want to make a cheap easy landing or small seating area you can lay railway sleepers as foundation and screw the decking directly to the sleepers *(naturally you will need to make sure the sleepers are levelled first)*. You can also add decking to the front of planter boxes to give that decking feel to a tiny space.

The secret garden: Many houses have outdoor spaces you can use as surprising value adders. For example, a narrow side path can be used to make a wonderful secret garden.

On more than one occasion I have put narrow double French doors in a bedroom to open it out into what was an unused strip of garden at the side of the house, *(you usually need about a five foot wide strip to make something really stunning, but you can do it with three or four feet at a pinch).*

I screen off either side, install a small deck, a large mirror, some plantings, hanging baskets, pots and a lovely garden bench. This is not an overly expensive exercise, *(if you are working on an older home you can often pick up the doors on eBay),* but the effect is totally magical. It gives a room that would otherwise have a very average view its own unique private garden.

Plants: If you are in a hurry, and don't have time to let your garden grow in, you may choose to go with more established plants, but doing this will come at a considerable cost. It will be far more economic to buy smaller plants and give them enough time to get established.

If you have a bit more time and the climate is suitable you can grow a wonderful garden for almost no cost by using cuttings and splitting roots, rhizomes and bulbs. Some plants that are particularly easy to propagate from cuttings are geraniums, pelargoniums, daisies, chrysanthemums, jade plants, practically any succulents, yuccas, agaves, and figs.

It is very easy to split the root ball of agapanthus, and the rhizomes of ginger or canna lilies and they make a great display. Bulbs like gladioli, irises and tiger lilies are also easy to split and multiply. You will need at lease 6 weeks to strike effective cuttings, and if you follow any of the many instructional videos on "You Tube" you should see about a 70-80% success rate (as long as you keep them watered).

If you are attempting to grow a lawn from seed, depending on the weather you will need at least 8-10 weeks to get it looking really lush. In some dryer climates, where garden water use may be restricted this might not be an option. In such places they will often allow you to water in freshly laid turf but they will not allow you to water up from seed. Choose a grass that is suitable to your location rather than one that you like, as if your grass is not suitable for your conditions it will never look good. While I love many of the soft fine grasses you can grow in the UK, I would not use them in a dryer climate like the South West of the US.

If you are planning to renovate and sell quickly you might want to grow some planters and hanging baskets that you can take with you. I have a stock of large potted plants, and hangers that I use to add a bit more pop to the gardens in quick flip properties.

A word of warning about trees and garden beds: Some trees have monster roots that can undermine your foundations and eat into your sewer pipes, so be aware of what you are planting and how invasive the roots can be. Willow trees, for example, are notoriously thirsty and their roots will smash through clay sewer and storm water pipes to get the water they need, and that can be a very costly repair.

If the house has any foundation problems, check if it is related to any nearby tree roots. If you have a large beautiful tree that is causing foundation problems it doesn't necessarily mean you have to loose the tree. It is possible to dig down and sever the roots that are causing the problem and install a root barrier. The tree will respond by sending its root out in the other direction.

Anything you plant directly next to a house has the potential to do damage if you do not plan it properly. Take particular care when planting raised garden beds next to a house. Raised garden beds should not interfere with proper sub floor or wall ventilation, so putting raised beds all the way around a property is generally a no no.

An exterior wall should never have dirt piled up directly against it, *(even if it is brick)* as this is likely to cause damp problems. If you want to use raised beds next to the house you will need to construct a frame that protects the wall. Once you have built your bed you may also want to waterproof and line the wall side with strong builders plastic to make sure no moisture is sitting near the wall of the house.

Drainage and stormwater: Depending on your topography you may have problems with standing water or storm water flows. This problem can be significantly more pronounced if your property is situated on a hill, or in an area where there are subterranean springs.

In most situations you will be responsible for making sure your storm water run off is properly discharged to the kerb and doesn't run into your down hill neighbours property. Storm water and drainage problems need to be addressed before you start building your garden so if you are renovating for sale you need fix any such problems immediately.

There are number of solutions to these problems, depending on your situation. If you have storm water that is sitting in pools and not draining off the property, the cheapest and most common solution is to install a dry well, or soak away pit. There a number of ways to install a dry well; if your water problem isn't too overwhelming then a simple DIY dry well can be constructed digging a deep pit at the point where the water pools and filling it with gravel. Unlike soil, gravel will not hold water. Water will drain easily through the gravel and soak down naturally into the water table.

If you have a larger volume of standing water to deal with you may need to put in more substantial dry well consisting of a reinforced concrete cylinder with perforated sides and bottom. This type of soak away can provide for some additional water storage while it slowly drains down into the water table. A concrete cylinder pit will need to be covered with a grate, whereas a gravel pit can be covered with a layer of soil and grass, which will render it practically invisible.

RECYCLING

In this throw away age it can be tempting to just strip out an old house and send it all to land fill. While that may seem like the quickest and easiest option it is not always that great for the planet. There is a lot of stuff that can be reused and repurposed with a little thought and effort.

Scrap metal yards will often come collect old taps, roofing tin, copper pipes, cookers, fridges and electrical wires. Your old kitchen, counter tops or cast iron bath could sell on eBay. Old fireplaces, windows, doors, floorboards, skirting, and architraves can be recycled through your local demolition yard. Many waste recovery centres have separate areas for dumping e-waste, appliances, metal, green waste, wood cardboard and paper. If it is at all possible to separate and recycle your trash, landfill should be your last option.

NEIGHBOURS

Dealing with neighbours during a renovation can be tricky. Your renovation can create a lot of noise, dust and traffic chaos that can block your neighbour's access and generally make their lives hell for the duration.

It is best to let your neighbours know of your intentions to renovate well ahead of time, giving them as much warning as possible. Give them a time frame, so they can feel comfortable that it won't drag on forever, and once you have started work make sure you give them a few days notice of any particularly loud or large machinery that may you may be utilising.

Most jurisdictions have some kind of noise restrictions that limit the hours in which you can operate loud machinery but even so it is still best to consult, you don't want to book your sand blaster for the same day as you neighbours birthday BBQ. Even if your local laws say you can do it, loud equipment on a Sunday morning is never going to win you any friends.

If your neighbours get their backs up they can make your life very difficult and cost you big money, so it can be a good idea to offer to do some small maintenance work for them in order to smooth over any tensions. For example on a recent job I painted out the graffiti in the back lane for all the neighbours. I had to have my back gates painted anyway, and it only took an extra hour for the painter, but it bought me a world of good will.

SAFETY

Site safety is crucial. Quite aside from any tragic human cost, if an accident should happen and the insurance company deemed that there were unsafe practices or inadequate safety provisions they may refuse to pay out, and that could be financially devastating. What ever you do don't scrimp on things like security fencing, proper scaffolding or harnesses. Make sure all trades people carry the proper insurance and when on site they are wearing the proper work attire, like closing shoes, high visibility vests, hard hats etc., as required by law.

Keep your site clean. Regular rubbish removal is essential. A build up of offcuts or demolition detritus is dangerous; the more trash that is laying around the greater the risk of accident or injury. Tripping and nail puncture wounds are extremely common on messy sites and can cause serious injury.

Have the necessary safety equipment to protect your self on hand. You will need, ear plugs/muffs, safety goggles, a good quality ventilating face mask, leather gloves, latex and rubber gloves, some kind of head protection, and sun screen (if applicable).

Have a well-stocked first aid kit. Your kit should have the following items on site at all times; antiseptic liquid and lotion, medical alcohol, small scissors, tweezers, cotton balls, surgical dressing and elastic bandages in a range of sizes, band aides, an eye bath, a sling (or fabric suitable to improvise), butterfly clips, surgical tape and a clean dish for washing wounds. Post an emergency services poster with hospital, ambulance and poisons numbers in a location that is clearly visible to everyone working on your site.

PART FOUR

SELLING HOUSES

PREPARING A HOUSE FOR SALE

The difference between the selling price of house that has been properly prepared for sale and one that has just been thrown on the market as is can be tens of thousands dollars. This is of course good news when you are buying a poorly presented property, but can be a financial disaster if you are selling one. Buyers will forgo a lot that is on their checklist if your home "feels" right, and a lot of the "feel" comes down to your presentation.

Selling an occupied house:

The first thing you need to do is de-clutter, the second thing you need to do is de-clutter, and the third thing you need to do is de-clutter! Clear out as much stuff as you possibly can. An overcrowded house will seem much smaller than it really is and that is a definite no no.

When clearing the clutter do not just open the fitted robes and shove stuff in. Buyers will inspect the robes to see what kind of storage they offer and if they are stuffed stupid this will send a clear message that there is not enough storage space. If you are short of places to put things and can't bring your self to get rid of stuff then hire a storage locker to keep it in while you are selling. If you have messy or difficult tenants it may be better to have them leave before you put the house on the market. Losing a month's rent can yield ten times that amount in an increased selling price.

Remove any personal photos, especially family pin boards and portraits. While you may think they make your place look homey, to buyers they make it look like somebody else's home. It is much easier for buyers to see themselves living in a house if they are not feeling the strong presence of another family. Put any confronting or challenging artworks, furnishings or decor items in storage, along with anything that represents an overly personalised taste that is unlikely to have broad appeal.

If you have any furniture that is looking dated, tired and unfashionable either remove it, or cover it. A simple tablecloth with a vase can be a design statement. A sofa can be covered with contemporary, neutral slip on covers, cushions and throws. I once dressed a sofa in calico off the roll held in place with safety pins, it cost less that $20 and it looked fabulous. If you have an old divan bed but don't have the right valance you can get a contemporary look by covering it with an inexpensive fitted sheet.

Often a coat of white paint or a lime wash will make old scruffy cheap pine woodwork look French provincial sheik. Cull any art works that don't match your colour scheme. You can replace them with wallpaper over canvas panels, or even get cheap frames from Ikea and do some colour co-ordinated potato cut prints. Get creative and improvise, it's surprising what you can do with almost no budget.

Clean everything. That means windows, cupboards, floors, cobwebs, fridge, oven, cooktop, baths, showers, basins, toilets, tiles, doors, door handles skirting, architraves and anything else you can think of. If you are not having new carpets for the sale then get the existing ones steam cleaned. Pressure clean the exterior of the home to remove any dirt, dust or old cobwebs, and pressure clean your rubbish bins to get rid of any lingering unpleasantness. If there are any old cars or machinery parked in the drive you need to either get rid of them or arrange to have them stored off site

Keep the place tidy. Keep the dishes done, laundry in the hamper, trash taken out, and no sand box ashtrays by the back door. If you have a pet bed, make sure it is clean and fresh and doesn't give off an odour and place it in the garage or outside during inspections. Counter tops and tables should not be home to any extraneous objects. While it may be a struggle to keep things in show home condition if you are living in the property it is important to keep all surfaces as clean and clear as possible.

Get the garden in order. Trim the lawns, chop back overgrown foliage, plant some coloured annuals, rake up any leaves, clear paths etc. Remove and replace any dead or sick looking plants and apply fresh mulch to the garden beds.

Make the house smell nice. This means no smoking inside, no overt cooking odours *(cookies and coffee are OK, but fried liver and Indian food are out)*, no unfortunate bathroom smells *(keep the air freshener handy),* and no old wet dog smells. You may want to put out some fresh flowers or a gentle oil burner, but keep it subtle, nothing too overpowering.

Selling an empty house:

Selling a house that is unoccupied is far easier in terms of presentation. While many people leave unoccupied houses empty for viewings it can be worthwhile having the house professionally staged.

Professional Staging

This usually results in a show home type presentation, which is very attractive to buyers. Most professional house stylists have warehouses of furniture and artwork so they are usually able to accommodate any type of house.

Professional staging can be expensive so you need to do your sums and work out whether it is likely to bring you a return.

If you can not justify the expense of professional staging you can still dress the house with one or two well chosen pieces of furniture, artworks, potted plants and a rug or two. This can be done on a tight budget and can add a great deal of homey ambiance to an otherwise empty place.

Get any mail diverted and put up a no junk mail sign to avoid getting inundated with catalogues. Put a few lamps on timers to give a more lived-in impression.

CHOOSING AN AGENT

Depending on where you are located an agent will charge you anywhere from 1.5 to over 6% of your selling price. The USA is the most expensive place to sell in terms of agent's fees as the buyer's agent will take their commission out of the selling price as well.

Higher fees do not necessarily equate with better service, but often those agents that charge a little more have a reputation for achieving a better price. If an agent offers to work for a fee that is well under the market rate for your area they may be banking on discounting your price for a quick easy sale and may not be prepared to put as much shoulder into getting you the best price.

Look at the agent's entire fee structure, including all advertising and promotional costs. Depending on where you are and what type of property you are selling this can add up to a significant sum of money. Check whether their price includes any applicable sales tax.

As I said earlier, it is well known in the trade that agents have to make two sales on every house. The first sale is when they get you to list your property with their agency. The second is when they sell your house to an actual buyer. It is important to remember that when an agent comes by to give you an appraisal that agent is also selling you their services, so take that into account when you are assessing what they have to say.

Finding a good agent is a lot easier if you have done your research. Go and visit other open homes in your area. Check the sold prices and days on market statistics. Many reputable agents will bring you a list of comparable sales in the area, so you can see for yourself what similar homes have been selling for. If you have selected someone to do your title transfers, contracts and legal work ask them who is a top seller in the area; they should know.

As with buying keep your cards close to your chest. Don't give away information that may be used to put you under any undue price pressure. If you are desperate for a quick sale don't let it show. Calmly let the agent know you would prefer to settle a sale sooner rather than later and as such you want to be realistic, but you are not in a desperate hurry and don't want to "give it away". If there is an active "market value" buyer out there, they will find your property within two to four weeks, and if they like it you will probably get an offer. You don't need to be screaming "fire sale" right from the get go.

Find out what your agent's vetting process is for people inspecting your home. Do they do open houses and if so do they require ID, or can anyone just wander in? Do they pre-qualify buyers for approved finance before they can book an inspection? What security do they provide for open inspections? How many agents will be present? How much notice will they give you before bringing someone through to view?

Will your agent actually accompany all viewers or just send them around to knock on your door? As a rule agents just sending people around for you to show through the property is not a practice I approve of. Unless you are a professional realtor you should not be expected to conduct viewings.

Viewings are an important part of the sales process and as such they are an important part of the agent's job. Also potential buyers will not feel as comfortable discussing the pros and cons of your house in your presence. It will be far more difficult for buyers to feel at home in your presence, as they will be acutely aware that it is YOUR home they are looking through. It is much better if you are not there at all when there is a viewing, and if you absolutely can't leave the house you should at least stay well out of their way and let the agent show them through.

Listing with multiple agents:

This is not something I tend to do. An agent that has exclusive selling rights will most times work harder to sell your property.

There are also some little known but quite real dangers in engaging more than one selling agent. There have been occasions where buyers have made initial enquiries with one agent, and followed up with another, leading the buyer's details to be registered with both agents. In such cases disputes as to which agent introduced the buyer have lead to vendors being forced to pay a commission to both agents.

In many places *(particularly the USA)* they have a multi listing system that will allow other agents to bring their buyers to your property, so listing with multiple agents doesn't necessarily confer any tangible benefit.

SETTING THE PRICE

Agents know that everyone wants the best price for their house, and as such it is common practice for agents to give a valuation that leans a little to the high side while they are selling you their services and pitching for an exclusive agency, *(this is particularly so in a balanced or sellers market).* Some less reputable agents will shamelessly inflate the promised price in order to get you to sign an exclusive agency and then start to massage your price expectations downward the moment they have you signed up.

Agents who don't list any prices on their advertising may be involved in over-quoting, *(using terms like "contact agent" where other agents list the price or price range).* When an over-quoting agent is signing you up you will be told your house is one of the best they have seen of it's type, popular and in demand. Only after they have locked you in will they will show you lists of other properties similar to yours that are on the market for considerably less and they will then present you with a long list of faults that are turning off potential buyers.

While an over-quoting agent won't necessarily sell your house for any less than an agent who has been more honest about the price you could realistically achieve, the process of having your expectations built up and smashed back down again can be extremely stressful and emotionally taxing. I always stress to any prospective agent that I want a REALISTIC appraisal.

While there is no problem with testing the top edge of your market value, there are dangers in overpricing your house at the start of a sales campaign. If an overpriced house attracts no interest owners will often be reluctant to reduce the price quickly and significantly enough to make it attractive to the active buyers in their market. Instead they reduce the price in small increments over a long period of time resulting in their property going stale on the market.

Assuming your realtor has priced and advertised your property correctly, the best price you will get offered for a house will quite often come in the first 2-4 weeks of a campaign, as everyone who is actively looking for your kind of property will find their way through your house within that time frame. If you do not get an offer from any of the active buyers in the first 4 weeks then you are stuck waiting for new buyers to enter the market. Meanwhile your property is falling further and further back in the web site listings. The agent will stop giving it their attention and will either move it to a less prominent position, or take it out of their window altogether to make way for fresh stock.

Most buyers who are new to the market look at the first few web pages of listings when working out which properties to go and view. Even if you have dropped your price down to a realistic level, if you are sitting on page 5-6, and they bother to look that far the question they will be asking themselves is "What's wrong with this house? Why hasn't anyone bought it already?" They don't realise that your price was too high when it first hit the market. They just see a house that appears to be correctly priced and that no one wants it. The assumption they will make is that there must be something very, very wrong with it.

I recently consulted with a property owner who found himself in this very situation. After being over-quoted he had slowly inched his price down from $710,000 to a more market realistic $535,000 but in spite of this his house had sat with only one or two viewings and not a single offer for seven months. He was so desperate to sell that he was preparing to drop his price to $480,000 in an effort to finally clinch a sale.

If you find yourself in this situation it can be worth changing agents, changing your copy, getting some fresh photos and re-listing it so it appears at the top of the relevant search listings. Getting fresh photos is absolutely crucial for exterior shots in places where the change in season is obvious. *(You don't want your listing to be featuring a shot with snow on the roof in September).*

In the above case the vendor engaged a new agent, had the copy rewritten, used a wonderful photo of the garden as a new lead image and put the price back up to $555,000. Much to the owners amazement this produced a flurry of new interest and he ended up selling his house for $548,500 within two weeks.

When setting the opening price research is key. Don't rely on your agent to tell you what the situation is, find out for yourself. Go and look at what is for sale, trawl though the local sold prices and get as good a picture of the market as you possibly can. A good agent will appreciate the fact that you have educated yourself and are realistic in your expectations, and they will reward you with their very best efforts.

If you are going to auction, you may not want to set your reserve price until after you have had feedback from viewings, but no matter what your situation there is not excuse for not pulling the recent sales prices for your area.

ADVERTISING

In some places advertising costs are practically non-existent; in other places it is a major source of income for realtors. While some agents will throw in floor plans and photos, others will charge you an arm and a leg. Australian capital city agents are the biggest offenders. It is not uncommon for a vendor to be asked to cough up advertising costs of $3-5k on top of the agent's fee, and I have seen it go as high as $25k for a top of the market property.

I would recommend getting good photos. Sometimes an agent will suggest they just snap a few photos themselves; and while I would let them do this to see what kind of results they get I would not hesitate to get professional photos taken if they are not up to standard. *(Do not, repeat, do not worry about hurting your agent's feelings if you choose not to use their photos.)*

Get a floor plan done; people like them. A floor plan gives buyers a chance to fantasise about what tweaks and changes they could make and you definitely want people engaging their imagination with your property. I have seen house hunters play with a floor plan for hours, *"you could move this wall"*, *"you could turn that area into another bedroom"* etc., by the time they actually go and view the property they are half way through the remodel in their head.

In my experience many realtors will offer you advertising packages with the major city mastheads and the local papers in your area. While these may have brought good results 15 years ago, these days newspaper advertising is more of an ad for the agency rather than your property. Unless you are marketing a property specifically to the over 65's newspaper ads no longer worth the money. Many agents have their own glossy magazines and will charge you a premium to be included. Generally I don't go for those magazines as they are really just advertising for the agency. In today's market anyone seriously about buying a property is looking online. Listing with the major websites is probably the cheapest and most effective advertising you can get.

PREPARING THE CONTRACTS

In some places you will be required to have a contract *(AKA as a vendor's statement or disclosure statement)* fully prepared before you can advertise your property for sale. This can take anything from a couple of days to a couple of weeks depending on what documents you are required to provide in your disclosure statement. Ordering the searches and assembling the documentation required is something your closing agent or solicitor/conveyancer would usually undertake for you.

Be aware that most of the required searches will cost money so you will usually have to pay the cost of the searches upfront.

Generally you will not be required to pay your closing agent until you have actually closed on a sale, but this can vary so ask up front for a schedule of services and costs.

Make sure you find out what costs you will be liable for in the event your property doesn't sell and in what time frame you will have to pay. This is particularly crucial in England where buyers are constantly making offers, starting the process and then pulling out of the sale. You don't want to be paying your solicitor every time someone makes an offer and pulls out.

As part of your disclosures you will usually be required to provide a list of fixtures and fittings that are included in the sale. This would usually include any fitted carpets, light fittings, blinds and curtains, TV antennae, satellite dish, clothes line and may also include things like the cooker, dishwasher, fridge, washing machine. Every jurisdiction has a different set of standard inclusions, so make sure you are clear on what is in and what is out. If there is something that is a standard inclusion in your area and you want to take it with you make sure you tell your agent and that it is clearly stated in the contract.

Let your solicitor know if you have any additional non standard clauses that you want included, such as a long or short settlement period, the right to remove a specific plant from the garden, or even the right to store things in the garage for an extra 2 weeks, etc.

If the property is being sold with tenants in place the contract needs to clearly state that the property is subject to a tenancy and will not be vacant at closing.

OPEN HOUSE OR PRIVATE INSPECTION?

There are two schools of thought on this and I am not firmly convinced one strategy is better than the other. Mostly it is something that is negotiated, taking into account the personal preferences of both the agent and the seller.

With a busy open house you will get quite a few tyre kickers and nosey neighbours, but you will also get serious buyers through the property. This can give buyers the impression that there is a lot of competition and prime them to act quickly, but it can also taint their impression in a negative way.

If there are a lot of people viewing the house at the same time it can make the place seem a lot smaller. It can also make moving through the house a lot more difficult and make the place appear less functional as a space. Generally buyers will not feel as comfortable and relaxed in the house if there are other people jostling all around them. A serious buyer cannot stand quietly and imagine themselves living in the house with a stream of people pushing to get past them.

On the other hand if you have an open house and only one party turns up, even if they love the house and are serious buyers the lack of other lookers may cast a shadow of doubt in their minds and it may effect any offer they are prepared to put forward.

There is also the issue of security with an open house. Things have been known to go missing, especially if your agent is not taking photo ID at the door.

Private inspections can be far more time consuming for the both the agent and the seller, but the agent will get to give quality time and attention to each buyer. With private inspections the seller will need to keep the house in a near show home state, ready for an inspection at a moments notice.

Private viewings offer a buyer a chance to interact with your property in a far more intimate way. The property will feel far more spacious and functional without twenty people in it and buyers will really be able to feel themselves in the space. Also potential buyers will not know how much other interest there is in the property, *(as they are there on their own)*, and this can give your agent a chance to create more of a sense on urgency in a potential buyer.

If you are able to leave the property during inspections this will give buyers the space to bring up any concerns with the agent and you will get more accurate feedback.

AUCTION OR PRIVATE SALE?

This choice will be largely dictated by what is common practice in your area and the circumstances under which you are selling. In most places a private sale, where you list a price and negotiate offers is the most common method of listing a property on the market. In a neutral or buyers market it is probably the best call.

If time is the primary consideration an auction is a good way to put a date on it, but it's is not a great strategy in buyers market. In many places it will mean taking a significant hit on the price. It is also worth bearing in mind that an auction may reduce your pool of potential buyers, as finance can be more difficult.

Another issue with auctions is that you will only ever get one bid above what the second highest bidder is prepared to pay. For example, consider the situation where there is a buyer who is prepared to pay $355K for a house, but the next highest bidder is only prepared to pay $320K. If that house went to auction the vendor would only ever get a bid of $321K, and not the $355K that buyer one was actually prepared to pay. In this scenario the seller would clearly have been better to have his agent negotiating a private sale.

If you have a highly desirable property and you are in a seller's market you may choose to sell through the sealed bid process, also known as sale by set date. This is more like a secret auction, where no one knows what anyone else is bidding. In the above example the vendor would have got the full $355k. In a hot market I have seen the sealed bid process produce unbelievable results.

SIGNING THE CONTRACT

As a general rule any cooling off period in a contract is for the buyer, not the seller, so it is crucial when selling that you have thoroughly reviewed the contract and know exactly what it is in it. Know what fixtures and fittings are included, the proposed settlement date *(although in many places this date is not set when signing the contract)*; check that any special conditions are accurately noted and that all amendments are initialled and dated.

If you are in anyway unsure, book time with your legal representative to step you through the contract and make sure that all agreements and requirements are clearly laid out before signing. For the most part you will be able to do this as soon as the contract disclosures are prepared, and you will only need to review any special conditions that have been negotiated between you and the buyer.

VACATING THE PROPERTY

A sale contract that is not subject to a tenancy is usually specified as a "vacant possession" contract. Unless there are specific inclusions in the contract like a fridge, or a couch etc., vacant means totally vacant. No old paint tins in the garage, no unwanted furniture, nothing. While most buyers are happy to have the paint tins left for touch ups, it is better to check rather than just assume. I have known buyers to delay settlement until touch up paint, left in good faith, was removed. I have also known buyers to demand money off the seller for "rubbish removal", which is a total pain if you have already moved away.

Technically you are obliged to hand the property over to the buyer in the same condition that it was in when they signed the contract, which means you may need to get the lawns mowed and the gardens weeded a day or two before.

You will also need to make good any problems that have arisen since the contract was signed. Which means any broken windows would have to be fixed, any graffiti removed, any tenant damage repaired; basically anything that has gone wrong since signing has to be made good.

I once had a house burst its main water pipe under the driveway two days before settlement was due. Under the terms of the contract I had to repair the pipe before we closed. This held up closing by a week, as I had to dig up the drive to make good the plumbing.

While I have never seen a sale contract that specified that the property be handed over clean, cleaning the property is the polite thing to do for someone who has just handed you a huge chunk of cash. There is nothing worse than picking up the keys to your new house and realising you have to spend the next few days cleaning it. So please, sweep, wipe, vacuum and put the bins out.

CLOSING THE DEAL

Once a time and date are locked in the buyer will often want to do a final inspection the day before, to make sure the property is in proper order. Once the buyer is satisfied that all is well, the seller then hands all keys to their selling agent and the legal teams of both the buyer, the seller, and their respective lenders will meet to settle the deal. Title deeds will be adjusted, seller's mortgages discharged and buyer's mortgages registered. Neither the buyer nor the seller is usually present at this meeting.

Once all the legal and financial work is complete the buyer and seller will be contacted by their representatives and informed that the deal has been done.

At that point the selling agent will make all keys available to the purchaser. After closure the seller no longer has any rights to be on the property, so anything you have left behind will be inaccessible without your obtaining the purchasers permission to come onto the property.

At this point you have successfully sold your property!

REFLECTING ON YOUR EXPERIENCE

Once you have successfully made it all the way from purchase, through renovation to a sale you will know for sure that you have what it takes to deal in property. You will know that you are stronger, more resourceful and resilient than you ever realised. You will no longer need to work nine to five if you choose not to and you will be able to live in a better house and make more money.

I wish you all success in the future and hope that your property dealings bring you everything you wish for. Good Luck on your journey!

Margaret.

Printed in Great Britain
by Amazon.co.uk, Ltd.,
Marston Gate.